OUT
OF THE
CLOSET
IN MY
MIND

Janet Manne

Vocamus Community Publications
Guelph, Ontario

Written by Janet Manne
©All rights reserved

ISBN 13: 978-0-9881049-3-8 (pbk)
ISBN 13: 978-0-9881049-4-5 (ebk)

Vocamus Community Publications
130 Dublin Street, North
Guelph, Ontario, Canada
N1H 4N4

www.vocamus.net

2014

Foreword

During a regular worship service the children were asked the question, "What would you like to be when you grow up?" Immediately the words formed on my lips without a hesitation, "A girl," but II dared not allow them to be heard, for everyone thought II was a boy.

Living in the closet II had created in my mind for most of my life gave me a sense of safety and protection. II was free to dream in there. II could hide in there, in the dark and quiet recesses, a lonely place, where only II had the key, and only II could enter.

II believed II was safe from the hurts, the pain and the fear of being different. II kept my secrets there with me, where they were safe and wouldn't be discovered. As II went through the many revisions writing this story, it became apparent just how empty and shallow my life had been before the walls of my closet suddenly collapsed and my secrets were catapulted out.

Part I

God, Where Did II Come From?

1
My Family's Legacy

The legacy my family left to me is best described as a ball of left over ends of wool from projects of love that had been tossed aside and hopefully forgotten. The ends, the knots, the tangles and the strands of many colours were rolled and entangled into a ball that no one wanted to unravel because they feared what might be found.

Because we live in families, our lives can, and often do, resemble a ball of messed up colors. Our lives become entangled with one another and the lives of family members who have gone before us. Their lies, their deceit, their deeds, their hurts, their pain and suffering, get hidden in family secrets. Combined with our own actions they create such tangled family dynamics, it's a wonder that some of us ever survive. Some family members possess the keys that could unravel these balls, but they won't let anyone have them. Why? Because they fear the shame that might be brought on the family. It's tragic that these secrets have been allowed to have such a disastrous affects on their own lives and on the lives of their family, that they have been compounded and carried into the lives of future generations.

In the past few years II have been forced to confront and deal with the legacy II have received. Fortunately, II have had the advantage of many friends who shared with me that II was not alone. They too have had their own legacies that have kept them in the bondage of fear and loneliness. Like me, they also tried to find safety and solace by locking the hurts and secrets in closets in their minds. Like them, II feared shame, rejection and what people would think of me. In the process of keeping my secrets hidden II allowed the pain, fear and shame to cripple my relationships with people, including my own immediate family. II allowed them to hinder my opportunity to live life abundantly. Perhaps you have experienced this emptiness in your life. The circumstances of your legacy are no doubt different, but it's not the circumstances that do the damage. It's the lies and deceit we use to cover them over. Eventually the timing was right for me to acknowledge and confront my hurting feelings and my fear of being different and to give these destructive secrets that had been crippling my life back to their rightful owners where they belonged. Then II was able to start house cleaning the closet in my mind, to rid myself of my lies and deceit and begin a journey of healing.

My maternal and paternal grandparents came from entirely different stock. Mom's family came from England, you know, the stiff upper lip type of folk, rooted in the traditions of the British army. Granny was born on a British army outpost somewhere in India. II have no idea where Grandad was born except that it was somewhere in England. There were six kids in mom's family, three boys and three girls. Grandad was a tall thin man, and II'm told he rather fancied himself a soldier of fortune, which kept him off fighting in one of those wars of the early twentieth century. While he was off satisfying his ego, his wife and children were at home fending for themselves.

In order for Granny to make ends meet while grandad was away, she had to rely on the kids and take in a boarder. We knew him affectionately as "Old Chuck", a bachelor, who repaired sewing machines for a living, walking and carrying his little bag of tools and parts everywhere he went. According to mom, had it not been for him, their family would have experienced even greater difficulty making ends meet. He took on the role of surrogate father, husband and my grandad.

The times Chuck and II spent together were extremely important to me. Saturdays were ours to share together. Every Saturday for years we either went to a movie or a picnic in the park to feed the swans. The Saturday matinee usually had a newsreel, a cartoon, a Buck Rogers serial and a Roy Rogers wild west feature movie, all for only ten cents. Chuck was my Grandad, even after my mom's dad finally came home from his wars for good.

It was then that Grandad's abuse of his family re-

5

sumed. II'm positive that's why my aunts and uncles all lived such dysfunctional lives, with two of the boys leaving home in their teens and never returning to see their parents. Grandad remains in my memory as an angry and disillusioned man sitting in the darkened living room alone, constantly telling me to be quiet and saying, "Children should be seen and not heard."

Granny on the other hand was a small quiet woman who loved to cook and bake special treats. II have wonderful memories from the times we went to visit at her house. Along the path leading to the side door wafted the sweet scent of lily of the valley. Opening the door we were greeted by the comforting smells coming from her kitchen. At Christmas the smell of turkey roasting in the wood stove, the flavour of peas cooked with mint, the rich moist almost black fruit laden Christmas cake covered in almond icing, and the Christmas pudding with rum sauce are my treasured memories of Christmas at Granny's. Whenever II visited her, she was never too busy for me to help her in the kitchen, mixing batter, spreading out cookies and rolling dough.

Dad's family were Pennsylvania Dutch heritage, a culture that kept feelings close to their chest, quiet, reserved and willing to share everything they had with those in need. He had an older brother and a younger sister. II never met my grandmother. She had died before II was born. My memory of her comes from an old photo showing her as a heavy set woman hanging clothes on the line, wearing dark rimmed glasses and her hair in a bun. My dad's aunt became my substitute grandmother. Our visits to her on the farm always began with a moist over-stuffed raisin cookie, the likes of which II've never been able to duplicate. Perhaps it was the love she had for children, because she never had any of her own, or perhaps it was that old wood stove in the kitchen that produced such a memorable delight.

Out in the barnyard she had an old tom turkey who had seen better days. He had the run of the farm, and he thought it was his kingdom. As ruler of the barnyard he bossed anyone he liked and challenged anyone venturing into his territory. When he decided to take after me with his wings flapping and his gobbling, all II could do was scream, yell and run, hoping that II didn't fall in that terrible barn yard. My aunt always came running to my rescue with her apron flapping, a pocket of those cookies for me and a scolding for the turkey. Like my other grandmother, she spent time with me in the kitchen. II was her little helper. She left me a legacy, a love of cooking, and her most important ingredient, love for people in your life.

Gramp was a quiet giving man who always seemed to be helping people in their time of need. He was a railroader, an engineer, and darn proud of it. II've heard stories of how he brought men home during the depression times, men who were down on their luck, hobos riding the rails across the country in search of work. At

Gramp's they could take a bath, sleep, eat and even get a fresh set of clothes. Whenever II went in his house, II could count on a large pot of navy beans and salt pork simmering in the deep cooker on the stove. Even now as II sit here, my mind conjures up the aroma of those beans simmering. No one was a stranger in his house. He was known up and down the tracks for his hospitality and refuge. When Gramp died, many of those men he helped were there to say thanks.

Like a lot of people II grew up with adopted grandparents who had a positive effect my own life and values. It would be nice if II could thank them for the love they so freely gave.

For thirty years mom and dad lived their secrets. That's when II found out that they had married after II was conceived. How sad that in all those years they never felt the freedom to publicly acknowledge and celebrate that special occasion in their lives, but when mom was young it was perilous times for an unmarried girl to be pregnant. Society didn't take kindly to "girls in trouble". Families tried to hush up these embarrassing family "situations" by explaining the disappearance of their daughter by saying, "Oh, she's gone to visit her aunt in another city for a small vacation," when in fact she had been sent to an unwed mother's home to have her baby with the expectation that she would give up her child for adoption. The family's reputation would remain unblemished, but the poor girl would carry that secret hidden in her heart for the rest of her life. II'm fortunate that mom chose the path she did.

Much later in life II was devastated when II learned that mom had also been the victim of family incest. As II learned more about who my mom and dad were and the difficulties in their lives, it helped me to understand in part why they never celebrated wedding anniversaries. It helped explain the apparent frigidity in their relationship all those years. It helped explain my mother's fear of intimacy and her inability to show affection. Even now that II'm an adult, when II tell her II love her, she simply acknowledges my expression with, "Okay." It also helped explain her dominance in the family. No one was ever going to take advantage of her again.

We lived in a railroad city during the era of the mighty giants, when railroading meant steam engines, smoke and soot. II don't think any other city could possibly have had as many different railroads running through it, six in all. The city was crossed, dissected and bisected by railroad tracks. There were so many tracks, it's no wonder Jumbo the giant elephant of Ringling Brothers circus was killed by a train as they were unloading and setting up for "The Greatest Show on Earth". The city was divided into four quadrants by the tracks, and that conveniently divided the social strata as well. The northeast and southeast were overall people, railroaders and foundry workers, the northwest the blue collars, teachers and business people, and the southwest the white collars, doctors and lawyers. When you were told you were from the wrong side of the tracks, it meant you were from the north and southeast corners. That's where we lived, in the southeast, bordered by two railroad repair yards, the Cheaspeak & Ohio and the Michigan Central.

Dad was a railroad mechanic on the Michigan Central, repairing the rolling stock and engines as well as being called out any time of the day or night for the derrick crews. He was a gentle giant of a man, quiet, passive, just like his father. His hands were large and strong. They looked like he was wearing baseball gloves on each hand. His hands dwarfed mine, even once I was an adult. His baby finger was the size of my thumb. That's maybe why he never disciplined us kids. That was left to mom.

There was one incident when II was three. II wandered off from home and headed towards the trains in the repair yard. When mom noticed II was missing, she frantically searched the neighborhood, and since the repair yards were only half a block away from our house, it didn't take long before she was at the tracks. She found me sitting on the track where they shunt the cars back and forth into the yard for repair. It was the longest walk home. Every step II took my mother wacked my bottom with a switch.

"WAR DECLARED," were the headlines the year after II was born. The second world war had begun, and the American industrialists were quick to seize the opportunity to capitalize on the need for war materials in

Europe. Our little city became vitally important to their war effort. The main lines of the American railroads ran right through our town, situated half way between the industrial plants of Detroit and the ships bound for Europe in New York's harbor. It was an ideal location for crew changes, rolling stock inspection, repairs, coal and water refueling. Nine miles south was a port on Lake Erie where the large lake freighters docked to offload their cargos of coal to heat our homes and fuel the railroads. A small local electric railroad shuttled the mountains of coal on the docks to the rail yards in town. This little railroad (the London and Port Stanley or L&PS) ran a passenger service consisting of one or two green electrically operated cars with hard leather seats and windows that opened by pushing them up. The cars gently swayed back and forth as they traveled along the tracks, and a fresh cool breeze blew in the open windows. It meant a great deal to families like ours who couldn't afford the luxury of a car. For a quarter each, we boarded the train and traveled the nine miles to the beach in the hot muggy months of summer for picnics on the sandy beach and a swim in the cool lake. Along the boardwalk there were casinos of pinball machines and souvenir stands. Occasionally we had a special treat, a cone of greasy french fries lathered with a watery type of ketchup and a cold drink of Macki's orange. Passenger service on the Michigan Central transported the Canadian forces training west of town to the transport ships in Montreal and New York harbors bound

11

for England

Dad and the fellows he worked with fought their own private war keeping the trains running in all sorts of weather and conditions. The frequent rail traffic led to increased repairs and derailments. A derailment meant that the derrick crews were called out at any time of the day or night to clear the main lines and get the wrecks back into the yards for repair so the heavily laden trains of tanks, trucks, guns and aircraft could be on the move again. It was a vicious circle for these guys. No sooner had they opened the main lines then they were expected back in the yards to complete the repairs. During these years dad wasn't home very much, and II guess we never had the chance to bond like II did with my mother.

Before the war mom struggled with her own personal problems, single, pregnant, ashamed and fearful of public scorn, but she had to work and help support her family. She was a sales clerk in the white goods department of the main street department store by day and a seamstress by night, altering new garments from the store, garments she herself couldn't afford.

During the months she waited for my arrival, she kept herself busy preparing for my arrival by knitting and sewing. She was so sure I was a girl. She was so positive. There wasn't a question or a doubt in her mind. Everything she created for me was white and pink or trimmed in pink, little knitted booties and bonnets and dresses carefully smocked. At last her waiting was finally coming to an end, and II was about to make my grand entrance and see what kind of folks II had been given.

Mom lay in the delivery room of the old general hospital. She once told me that II wasn't coming out without a struggle. She says II caused her a great deal of discomfort and distress. Finally the nurses exclaimed that my head had crowned.

"Push," they kept encouraging her, "Push," and there II was in all my moist and naked glory.

"It's a boy!" proclaimed the doctor (No, he hadn't mistaken the umbilical cord for something else. II had that too.) and with that my mother began to sob. She had been so sure II was a girl. She was extremely disappointed.

2
Childhood Dreams

When II was growing up there was a photo hanging in Granny's bedroom of me dressed as a little girl standing in her garden. II never thought much about it until II started to find out more about who II really was. Through some family members II learned that for a while mom nurtured me as her daughter. Then one time when II was rummaging through a bunch of old boxes in the attic, II came across one labeled as my baby clothes. This sparked my curiosity. There they were, my little outfits, little dresses with their smocking and ribbons, the booties and blankets carefully wrapped in tissue.

As II grew up there were only girls my age in the neighborhood to play with, so naturally my playmates were girls, especially my cousin who lived next door in Gramp's house. Although she was a couple of years younger than me, we grew up more like sisters. My other playmates were the girl across the street and the girl who lived in the apartment above ours. We had great fun playing house and dolls. Playing house in the fall was especially fun because we could arrange the leaves in the yard and make a whole house with different rooms. We had tea parties with our babies and took them for walks up and down the street in their carriages. II remember my carriage was a brown wicker one with large wheels that had two round glass windows in the side of the hood. My baby was dark skinned. Maybe this was a forecast of the discrimination II would learn to face later in life. We had great fun dressing in our mothers' old clothes, shoes and jewelry and pretending we were grown up ladies.

Fall was always a beautiful time of the year. The pungent smell of burning leaves enveloped the city. It's a smell II still remember and miss because it signaled a special time of the year when we would go to country church turkey suppers, gather walnuts for the winter, and enjoy the smell of chili sauce emanating from the kitchen into the neighborhood through the open windows.

When II was about four, mom and dad sent me off to Mrs. Johnson's nursery school. This was a really difficult time for me every morning to be separated from my friends and my mother. Mrs. Johnson had a problem with me. She wanted me to play with the boys, but no matter what she did she couldn't change my preference to play at the girls' activities. Thank goodness it was only a year.

Then II was off to kindergarten with my friends from the neighborhood. Now II was really in trouble. Because II had been to the nursery school and pretty well knew the things they were trying to teach, II became bored and listless. They didn't know whether to keep me in the kindergarten or move me to grade one, and so they bounced me from one class to the other. Finally II had kicked up so much fuss in grade one that they felt my social adjustment was stunted, and II ended up back in kindergarten for the year.

The poor teacher had a difficult time trying to change my gender role, because II still preferred the girls' activities in class and at recess. In those days boys and girls were kept separated. Boys went in one school door, girls in another on the other side of the school. The playground was divided by an invisible "do not cross" line that ran from the steel circular fire escape slide to the fence. That didn't stop me. Before long II was with my two friends on the girls' side of the playground playing skip or hop scotch. There were those dreaded monitor teachers who kept peace in the school yard and kept the boys separated from the girls. It didn't take them long to spot this kid wearing corduroy breeks (horrible knee length pants that bulged at the sides and had to be worn with knee high wool socks that smelled terrible when they got wet in the rain and snow). II just wasn't comfortable on the boys' side of the school yard.

School wasn't a pleasant place for sissies. II was called names, bullied and made fun of. II grew up hating to go to school, and my grades reflected my attitude, barely scraping through from one grade to the next.

17

In those days of the war each child received a small bottle of milk at recess time. As II got a little older II began to stay on the boys' side of the imaginary "do not cross" line, drinking my milk and talking to my friends on the other side of the line. If we crossed that line we were bound to get the strap, and II couldn't afford to have red puffy eyes in the school yard or when II got home. II realize the strap is not in fashion in the school system today, but in those days it was used frequently. On one occasion II got it just for running up the stairs. It was a humiliating experience, standing in front of the class with the palms of your hand turned upward. Whack, down comes the leather strap on one palm, and while that palm is stinging, down comes the strap on the other hand.

For nearly six years II was an only child, and II had my mother's full attention most of that time. II guess we bonded closer than II did with dad. Unfortunately dad had a job that required a lot of hours and extra overtime hours, and so II really don't have many memories of him until II was in my early teens. Except for discolored photos in family albums II dare say there would be little to remind me that he was present in my life all those years.

Following the birth of my first sister, my relationship with mom distanced. She now had a real daughter. We still spent a lot of time together as she taught me how to sew and bake and help around the house, but the relationship had changed. II felt that she kept me at a distance.

A year or two later we bought a new house, still in the south east section of the city, a red brick two storey. It seemed so huge in comparison to the apartment. It was closer to the school, but it meant moving away from my close friends and playmates. II felt like II was losing everybody in my life, my mom and my friends all at once.

The new neighborhood was terrible, with mainly boys to play with. They were rough, constantly playing war games, or baseball, or hockey. We lived near a ravine where they built forts, started grass fires and played in the dirty foul-smelling creek that would sometimes have a coating of white oil that came from the foundries a few blocks away. They all had the same first name as II had, so everybody had to have a nickname. II had wire rimmed glasses, so they called me Four-eyes. II was also the smallest and the neighborhood sissy, so they called me Bird. Today II would be called a geek, nerd or faggot. II hated being called Bird. II thought it meant bird brain. Of course, at that age II would never have thought to associate it with the majestic grace of a soaring eagle.

For a year or two on Saturday mornings some of us kids in the neighborhood went to dance classes. A man and his wife who lived close by had turned the upstairs area of a large barn on their property into a dance studio. There were eight to ten of us, mainly girls and a few of us boys, who spent a couple of hours each week learning

19

to square dance and waltz. Sometimes the guys from the neighborhood would heckle us by shouting names as we practiced or ran home after a lesson.

II tried to cultivate friends with both the guys and the girls in the neighborhood, but frankly II preferred to be with the girls. With them II was comfortable, playing house, dolls, dress up, skip and hop scotch, but when the boys came around II was in trouble if they caught me playing with the girls. They ridiculed me, beat me up and generally despised me. Already II had begun building a closet in my mind and was being pushed inside.

Five years after my first sister was born we had another sister. Mom now had her two girls, and II began to feel that there was no place for me in the family. It was the beginning of the slippery slope of a poor self image. II even imagined myself dead. They would be sorry then, II thought. In my closet II fantasied a lot about my death, a fantasy that has remained with me throughout my life and one that I tried to make into a reality a few times. II don't accept rejection very well, and II didn't like what was happening to me. Instead of accepting the changes, II rejected them, as well as the people involved, and II withdrew into my mental closet where no one could hurt me.

II was known as the neighborhood sissy, and II became the target for bullies. One particular day II was chased home by one of the school bullies. II ran up onto the porch where II expected to escape into the safety of the house. As luck would have it, dad was home that day and was standing on the other side of the screen door. He latched the door when he saw me coming.

"You're not coming in here 'til you knock his block off," he snapped at me. Slowly I made my way back down the steps. The other boys were shouting, "Fight! Fight!" For boys fighting is a spectator sport. They seem to enjoy watching someone being brutalized. Once II had been punched and wrestled to the ground, someone pulled us apart. That's when II made a bee-line for the back door. II knew mom would be in the kitchen and II could escape straight to my room and the safety of my clothes closet. II hid in there the rest of the day, afraid to face dad. What II didn't realize was that he had already left for work, so II feared for nothing, but II still didn't come out of my room until the next morning to go back to school and face the hazing. After that episode II never defended myself by fighting. Instead, II just fell to the ground into a fetal position and covered my face with my arms. It didn't stop them kicking or piling on top of me, but at least they couldn't get a good swing at me.

It was about this age when the girls who had been my friends suddenly didn't want me around them any-more. They had reached the age where all boys somehow develop "cooties". Now II had to try and fit in with the guys, but II couldn't. II was always last pick for any game. II couldn't throw a ball like they did. II didn't run like they did. II couldn't hit the ball like they did.

Football was too rough. Besides who wants to get ground into the dirt? II couldn't skate. War games were no fun. II hated the thought of killing, and besides II didn't like getting dirty.

The only things II was good at were helping mom around the house and drawing. Mom and dad decided to encourage me with my art work by sending me to study painting with the resident artist at the girls' finishing school in town. II spent seven years being tutored there. Once in a while another boy would begin but would soon quit because all the other students were girls. II finally had something and someplace where II felt good, someplace where II didn't have to compete with the boys or my sisters.

In my early teens dad thought it would be a good idea for me to join the Boy Scouts. Perhaps they could make me more of a boy. In those days there was a pecking order among the guys in the troop – oldest, biggest, strongest and weakest. Unfortunately, like most things in my life, II fell into the least desirable category. II was constantly hassled, teased and picked on by the bullies from school and the neighborhood who also attended scouts. At times it was unbearable. II enjoyed hiking and camping, but some of the rituals we younger and weaker guys had to endure on these outings were terrible and degrading. II couldn't quit. Dad had this "thing" – if you started something you finished it. His philosophy became so ingrained into me that it has stuck with me almost to the ruination of my life.

Scouting held one advantage for me being a loner. Although it's based on teamwork, there is ample opportunity to be an individual achiever. II could work alone to achieve badges and awards. Soon II had more than any other guy in the troop and quickly rose through the ranks to junior leadership. As a junior leader II was exempt from the hazing. II had status in the pecking order.

It was the first time II remember dad becoming active in my life. He became part of the father's group and began taking part in our hiking trips. Dad also began to get me interested in working with wood. It was one of his pastimes. II think he developed his interest from his uncle, who was a cabinet maker by trade, with only two fingers left on one hand and four on the other. Mom was always on edge when dad and II were in the basement working with the tools. She threw a fit when she heard his big table saw start to whine like the propellers of an airplane as it rotated up to full speed.

The late forties and early fifties were boom times for the Simpson's and Eaton's catalogs. They were my dream books. II poured over them carefully, with secret desires to have the nice clothes shown for girls and women, but II dared not be caught looking through those areas of the catalogs. Someone might think II was weird, well, weirder than II already appeared to be.

Then there were the gym classes. During the winter months we went to the YMCA near the school for

23

swimming. The Y had a rule prohibiting bathing suits in the pool. II hated these classes. II was always made fun of by the guys because they had for the most part gone through puberty. II was the brunt of ridicule, simply because II hadn't, and II became the likeliest target for towel snapping.

As II was about to graduate from high school many changes were taking place. II was finally going through puberty. Sex was a taboo subject around our home and in the media. The teens at school thought they knew all there was to know from locker room discussions. Parents were embarrassed by it. Teens were preoccupied with it. II was shamed and embarrassed by it.

It was the fifties, the generation of rock and roll, the era of Elvis, the Everly Brothers, Fats Domino, Bill Haley, the sound of guitars and the prediction that the youth of the day would be the moral decay of society. Values were beginning to change. Gay culture was just emerging from its closet. A news release from Sweden reported that a man had undergone surgery to become a woman. The news filled me with a dream, but society and the Christian church reacted to these things with homophobic fears that escalated into violence as churches brought on religious persecution. Males who appeared the least bit feminine were immediately suspected of being a "fag" or a sexual deviant.

In high school II was given the nickname "Deviate", simply because II was different. II don't think any of them really knew how II felt inside. II ached from the pain of being different and an outcast. The fact that II saw myself as a girl, well, that was my secret. The cost of that secret meant that II had few friends, and not one of them would II dare share my feelings with, especially not with my parents.

II had taken electrical shop in high school. II remember my teacher telling me II would never be an electrician because II didn't want to get my hands dirty. His assessment was absolutely accurate. II didn't like to get dirty.

Because II was working at several part time jobs, II was fortunate to be able to buy an old car that needed constant repairs. The other guys in the neighborhood didn't have cars. Since II did, II suddenly became more acceptable, or perhaps it was the car. Anyway, they loved to tear down and work on my car. That suited me just fine. II got my car repaired, and they got to drive where they wanted to go. The car gave me a measure of acceptability. In my adult life this translated into feeling acceptable to others only when II had something they wanted or needed. II learned that tolerance could be purchased if II was willing to pay enough.

Dad started having serious discussions with me about where II was going to work. He had already sensed the writing on the wall concerning life on the railroad. He felt that its day was coming to an end with the advent of the trucking industry and other technology. The romance of the steam giants was being replaced by diesel engines.

He saw the railroads turning to technology to cut costs, requiring fewer workers. He felt strongly that my future lay in getting an education in automation, which was the buzz word of the late fifties. Unfortunately, nobody thought to tell the colleges what automation should or could mean. Everything was labeled automatic – door openers, can openers – but the colleges hadn't caught up with the times.

II found a college in Toronto that claimed it had a course in automation, so in the fall after graduating from high school II registered in this course. II began to realize after a couple of months that II was in over my head. With five subjects in chemistry and only a background of high school general science, II was hopelessly bogged in the mire. The longer II went to the classes the deeper II sank.

Needless to say, II failed that year, but the year wasn't a total failure. II found out what automation wasn't, and I met some girls who were studying microbiology in the same building. The more II learned about their course of study the more interest II developed.

II sold my car to pay my tuition and returned to college in the fall, entering a program called Laboratory Technology. II was sure this was my field. II had finally found a school program II thoroughly enjoyed. Some might think it a problem, but of about thirty students there were only two of us guys, and the other fellow dropped out after a few weeks. My grades were excellent. II couldn't get enough of the microbiology labs and theory. Then at Christmas, as II discussed with dad my enthusiasm for the course and the type of work it would lead to, he became upset. He couldn't see any future for me in a predominately female occupation working in a hospital medical lab. Since he was helping me financially, he cut the assistance, and there was no way II could continue my studies. A part time job wouldn't have been sufficient to support me.

After leaving college in January, II got a job with the Ontario Department Of Highways as a chain man on a survey crew, not the type of job for an indoor person, working outdoors in January and February. It was cold, snowy and wet. Two months was enough.

A friend of my dad was a union organizer who was just unionizing a new plant in the city of Galt. II had heard of this city through the neighbors who lived across the street. II called the plant and was scheduled for an interview the next day. Since II had sold my car to go to school, dad offered to drive me to the interview. That same day II had a job in the factory starting the next Monday, so II needed to find a place to live. Since II had no car, II needed to choose a place close to the plant. Fortunately II found a place boarding with a family, but II had to share a bedroom with their ten year old son. II really didn't see a problem with this, because II thought it would only be temporary. After all, II would soon be making good money, and then II could afford a place of my own. Things didn't exactly work out the way II had planned, and II ended up boarding with this family for several years.

After we had settled everything, dad and II decided to explore the city before we returned home. In the downtown area we came across an old time grocery store that sold sauerkraut in bulk, right out of a wooden barrel. For us this was a real treat, because we both loved sauerkraut, especially fried. The smell was making our mouths water as we drove home along the highway. We started to nibble it raw out of the container. By the time we arrived home we had finished the container and the car reeked of sauerkraut.

With a job in another city and no car, II decided II needed to bite the bullet and purchase a car before the weekend. II had my mind set on getting a two seater convertible sports car, one of those sporty English ones, preferably an MG, but since dad had to co-sign the loan from the credit union, he exercised his authority over the choice of cars. II ended up with a brand new brown, four door, six cylinder, automatic Ford family car, with a green interior, very practical and very boring for a twenty year old. My life has always seemed to be controlled by others because II have yielded to the decisions they made, whether or not II agreed with them or not. II always believed that by keeping quiet II saved a lot of hassles and conflict, but my silence carried a tremendous personal price.

My employment with the plant in Galt was short and not so sweet. I guess I had lived a sheltered life. I wasn't prepared for the macho male shenanigans that went on in that factory. I was a wet behind the ears youngster, who had never been exposed to the world of factory work. I learned that informers in the plant who reported the causes of production slowdowns to management were punished severely by their union brothers. One man was hung on the automatic paint line. Another had his chest sanded with a power palm sander. Management was tough too. When posting a speed limit in the parking lot didn't slow people down, the plant manager took it upon himself to have a ditch dug across the driveway, and then he stood there at quitting time with a sadistic grin on his face watching the people hit their brakes and the ditch.

After a few weeks I knew this wasn't the work environment I wanted, but Dad had always encouraged me never to quit one place of work before I had another job. After a few months of enduring this environment I was able to secure a job as a clerk in the engineering department of a company manufacturing electric motor controls.

This was a fantastic company to work for. They had confidence in their employees and encouraged them to continue their education through night classes. They even paid for the courses if we completed them successfully. With their help I was able to return to night school and obtain the college level courses that eventually allowed me to move from clerk to system designer and sales consultant. This company prepared me for my career in automation.

After a number of years' experience in this company, II decided to accept a position with one of their customers where II could expand the design and sales aspects of my career. They were a leader in their field and wanted to be on the cutting edge of automation technology. The new company doubled my income, provided a car allowance and offered profit sharing.

The first day II was introduced to the owner and president of the company. Our meeting was blunt and to the point.

"We've hired you because of what we think you know and what you can do for our company. We'll know in thirty days if we're right."

There was no ambiguity in this man's statement. II had thirty days to prove my worth. For the next nineteen years II worked along side this man of integrity, forthrightness and excellent business knowledge. Under his tutelage every person in the company had the opportunity to realize their full potential without being exploited.

II have never been satisfied unless there was a mountain to climb or something that pushed me to the limits of my ability. With this company II scaled mount Everest, but my drive has also been one of my downfalls, and many times II have fallen as low as II have risen.

II had a sign on my office wall.

"A person who never fails is a person who has never risked trying."

Throughout my life II found the encouragement II needed to go on from this simple saying. II have had my share of failures, II dare say. There were those times when my failures were whoppers, when only a good old fashioned pity party would suffice, but eventually II had to accept the wisdom of the sign. It was during the pity parties that II believed everything that went wrong was of course my fault. These negative thoughts didn't roll off of my back. II held on to them and added them to an already overstuffed bag of garbage II chose to carry around with me. Just stuff it in. Soon it will go away. But it never did.

Since II would spend the greater part of my career with this company and progress up the ladder about as far as the ladder extended, II guess my failures were only monumental in my own eyes. When the company was put up for sale, II took the opportunity to purchase the rights to one of the products II had helped develop and struck out on my own.

Part II

Hi, God! There's a Pit in My Cherry Pie.

3
Closet Living

Shortly after II had begun work at the new company, a young woman began working there for the summer before entering nurses training in the fall.

We were assigned to work together for the summer to complete a specific project. After a couple of weeks she started to bring in home made cookies and muffins for our coffee breaks. Pretty soon not only were we having coffee breaks together, but she began bringing in special lunches for us to share as we picnicked in the sun on the grassy areas around the plant. Finally II had a friend just like the old days. Here was someone II could sit and talk with. Towards the end of summer II thought it would be nice to spend some time together outside of the work environment, and so II invited her out for a coffee. This became a weekly ritual, going to the same restaurant for coffee and dessert or a sandwich. Each time II took her home, II simply walked her to the door, returned to the car and drove off.

The project we had been assigned to work on through the summer was nearly complete and way ahead of schedule. One morning a mishap set the project back and made it unlikely it would be completed on time. A couple of years later, she related how she had sabotaged our work that summer fearing she would be let go before the end of summer if the project was completed too early. When her summer work term ended, several months passed before II contacted her again to go out for coffee. Now that she was in nurses training, the first year students had a nine o'clock curfew from residence, so we barely had time for coffee when we went out. She told me a few months later that every time we came home the other girls in her class teased her about me simply walking her to the door and leaving her there.

One night she had enough of my unusual behavior and promised herself and her classmates it was tonight or never. When II walked her to the door, II didn't realize all the other girls in residence were waiting to see what would happen. When we arrived at the front door she suddenly said,

"Aren't you going to kiss me good night?"

(It had never occurred to me to do so.)

Then she wanted to know if there was something wrong with her.

Of course not, she was attractive, fun to be with. The problem was with me. II had just never been attracted to girls, and II never felt attractive to girls. II tried to do what II guessed was expected and gave her a peck on the cheek. She later told me II treated her like a sister. She

36

wasn't letting go at that. She planted a kiss squarely on my lips, and a cheer rose up from her classmates hanging out the windows. As II left her at the door that night and returned to my car, II was confused and embarrassed.

As the months went by II became more comfortable with the intimacy, and yet something felt wrong. Our relationship was developing, but she became impatient with my slow lead. She began suggesting that she leave nursing so we could get married. Things were moving far too fast. II wasn't even sure that marriage was for me, but the more II talked to her and the more she talked to my mom, the more II was being backed into a corner of honor by both of them.

II reasoned that she was a woman who had sacrificed a lot to go back to school and prepare herself to become a nurse, and now for the sake of marriage she wanted to throw it all away. II began feeling responsible for her, taking ownership of the decisions she was making. II tried compromise. Perhaps engagement would satisfy her for the time being, at least until she graduated in two years. For a short time it did offer some security to her, but then we were soon back to square one. Now she was half way through her training, and II couldn't imagine why anyone would chuck everything at that point, simply to get married.

In personal relationships II have been a procrastinator. If II didn't express my feelings or hear what II wanted to hear, II just hoped that the problem would disappear. For most of my life II practiced this twisted thinking, trying to avoid confrontation or hurting people's feelings no matter the cost. By keeping quiet II assumed responsibility for and took possession of the decisions other people made about their lives rather than face the guilt, the hurt and the confrontation II feared might take place if II spoke out. II effectively turned control of my life over to other people, while II stuffed my feelings into another dark corner of my closet.

Until this time student nurses were never given permission to marry during their training. II felt II could procrastinate another year and she could finish her training if II told her that we could only proceed if she got permission to get married in her third year.

The next morning following coffee break the phone rang. When II picked up the receiver she screamed,

"I did it! I got permission, and we're getting married in August!"

Again II had lost control of my life simply by allowing other people to make my decisions for me. We were married that summer, and she graduated the next year. Our first son was born a little over a year after we were married.

By the time our third son was born, our relationship was experiencing some real difficulties. II found myself living in my closet with my secret feelings. II had hoped that they would disappear with marriage and family. Instead, as the years went by, my feelings simply kept getting more and more fixed in my mind. Our disagreements became more frequent, and our intimacy suffered. II knew the cause, but II couldn't admit my problem. She was skilled at expressing her feelings, sometimes rather sharply, causing me to feel like II had been carved up like a roast of beef. II couldn't respond. Silence became my defense. II curled up in a fetal position hiding in a dark place. My actions, II admit, were child-like, hiding for hours in a clothes closet or under the stairs. II just couldn't stand up to her. My insecurity and fear of confrontation froze any backbone II may have had.

II knew II was failing as a husband and that she deserved more than II was able or willing to give. II felt like a failure as a father. II had this overwhelming belief that II would not see my thirty-second birthday. II can't explain why. It was just a strong impression constantly going through my mind, but that birthday passed, and so have many since.

II had a good job. We had a nice home. We had five children now. Materially we had the ideal life. The missing element was a loving relationship between two people, a relationship one assumes will constitute a fairy tale family. The problem was mine. II perceived myself as a social misfit, and consequently II withdrew deeper into my closet.

Socially II needed and wanted to withdraw from people. II found social gatherings uncomfortable. II didn't care to listen to the "heifer dust in the bull pit", the

39

one-up-man-ship of male conversation, their cars, their investments, or their sexual conquests and fantasies. II much preferred to spend time with the women and usually joined in their conversation. This was mistakenly interpreted as flirtation by my wife, resulting in accusations, which if she had really known the truth about me, would have seemed ludicrous to her.

II was working now for a company that liked being on the edge of technology. That balance point is very precarious between success and risk. Too many successes permitted larger projects requiring larger capital and generating larger worries. II became insecure in my ability, but II couldn't admit it to anyone. The more insecure II became the larger the risks II took. It was as though II was trying to create a situation that would justify my failure.

So far things were working out fine as far as the company was concerned. We were successful. Those II worked with didn't surmise the pain II felt or the doubts II had about my capabilities or the risks II was subjecting everyone to. At times it was like sitting atop an overturned boat that was sinking slowly, watching the sharks circling, knowing it was not a matter of if but of when II would become their next meal.

Every hour II was awake II was walking on a knife edge that II had created. It didn't seem to matter if II was at work or home. Every word, every action had to be carefully scrutinized. Who on earth could II share my feelings with, especially when II was being told at home that II wasn't to live by my feelings?

To me, this was impossible. My feelings were with me every hour of the day and night. They influenced my waking thoughts and actions. They impacted my dream state. II felt as though II was slowly losing my mind. II knew who II was, and II knew who II wanted to be, but there was no way to release my pent up feelings and emotions.

II tried to find some outlet by partially cross dressing under my working clothes, to try and feel somewhat feminine, but thoughts of my death still visited me more and more frequently.

My job was requiring more and more time away from home. II remember one trip where the fellows II was with decided we should all go to a strip bar. II never lived that experience down. While they were enjoying the show and their attention was absorbed elsewhere, II had quietly gone to sleep from sheer boredom. Female nudity didn't grab my attention.

II tried to hide my daily pain from myself with alcohol. II drank coffee constantly, at least that's what most people thought II was drinking. Actually it was coffee and vodka, and hold the cream and sugar please. One morning on my way to work II skidded on some ice and wrapped the tail end of my wife's Ford Pinto around a hydro pole. It was my wake up call that II hadn't really accomplished or solved anything with my special blend of coffee.

My relationship with my wife was deteriorating quickly. She was unhappy. II was unhappy. We were making the kids unhappy. By now she had become involved with a women's Bible study group. She had always had a much deeper spiritual side to her life than II did, but it seemed the longer she attended these studies the more she tried to point out the errors of my life. II would come home and find books left open to a certain page for me to read or to a taped message from a preacher on the Christian radio station for me to listen to.

She commented frequently that she believed there was a deep dark secret in my life that II needed to deal with. She had an amazing insight, but fortunately not the knowledge of what secrets my closet held. How could II possibly release a secret like mine? My personal secrets were the beginning of yet more destructive family secrets. She began to encourage me to take an interest in spiritual things and invited me to a couples Bible study, very slickly done II might add. The husbands of the wives in the Bible study were invited to an innocent pot-luck supper so we could all get to know one another. Shortly the discussions took on the nature of spiritual reflections, and soon we were discussing biblical passages. What was to have been a social outing became a weekly get together for coffee at one of the homes. Now what husband would be willing to risk being the first to drop out?

Next she suggested that we should seek help from the pastor of the Baptist church where her friend attended. Believing it would ease some of the tension, II agreed to give it a try, but II didn't hold much hope for solutions. As usual II agreed to attend only because II didn't want another disagreement.

What II feared most happened. The sessions focused on me. II was portrayed as a workaholic who was constantly listening to "the wrong tapes playing in my mind." The solution was oh so simplistic, but not easy. The pastor had no idea of the secrets II held in my closet, and yet, he felt all II needed to do was "change the tapes." II must have seemed like a workaholic because II didn't want to be home and subjected to the constant criticism of my spiritual life.

Every Friday II could take heart knowing that Monday was coming. Weekends were the worst times of my life in those days. Every counseling session ended with me being at fault. Everything that was wrong in our relationship was because of my wrong actions and thinking. Imagine what that pastor would have thought if II had told him how II really felt, that in reality II was a woman in a man's body. Needless to say the counseling sessions didn't work, and the miracles my wife was looking for didn't happen. II didn't give anyone permission to enter my closet.

Over the years attending these couple club Bible studies my heart softened to spiritual matters, as did those of several other husbands. II began going back to the church we had been married in and started taking a more active role in the church. On the other hand, II was feeling worse about myself, because II was sure God didn't want me living in the manner II was. The more II studied the scriptures the more II felt like there was a great deal wrong with me, but II never found out how to rid myself of these feelings. Prayer wasn't working. If God loved me so much why wasn't II getting answers? Why wasn't II being restored? Why did II still feel like a woman?

About this time we attended a week long Bill Gothard seminar in Toronto. The seminar dealt with many issues of life from a biblical perspective. His teaching sounded good, sounded correct, from what little knowledge II had of the Bible. Near the end of the seminar he made a statement that caught the ears of both of us: "If you're not in a Bible believing, Bible teaching church, get out, for the sake of yourselves and your family."

During the coffee break my wife and II looked at each other, and we knew we had to do something. The church we were attending in our opinion didn't fall into this definition. Oh, it used biblical passages in the service, but the sermons taught humanistic theology about spiritual matters. It had even begun ordaining women and homosexuals into the ministry. From what we were learning in the Bible studies, we believed this was in direct contravention of God's word. Homosexuals were living in sin and women were to remain silent in the church. The

Sunday school had become a baby and child care service while the parents were in church Our children were reading comic books instead of Bible stories because the church hadn't provided teaching materials. Everything II was learning about God in my own life was in my opinion being disputed by the church. II now realize how far we had stretched some of our interpretations.

Shortly after that, II made a business trip to Buffalo. It was a wet miserable day. The windshield wipers were sweeping back and forth. II was in a very down mood. II probably shouldn't have been driving that day because my mind certainly wasn't focused on the road as II sped along the busy four lane highway. II had the eerie feeling that there was another person with me, and yet II was alone in the car. As the miles passed, so too my life passed in review through my mind, all the deceitful things II had done, all the lies II had told. II was extremely depressed. II hated myself. II hated my life. II wasn't even a person, at least that's how II appeared to myself.

II was approaching Vineland on the Queen Elizabeth Way when II thought II heard a voice call, "Jacob." Again II heard, "Jacob." II remembered reading about a man named Jacob in the Old Testament. He was depicted as a schemer and a deceiver. Was that who II had become? Was II losing my mind? As II continued driving, this unseen presence was bringing to my mind all of the deceit and lies in my life before me. Was II hallucinating? II was becoming more and more depressed, feeling more and more like a worm.

At the garden center there was a concrete bridge that crossed a small stream running into the lake. My eyes were filled with tears. My spirit was broken. On an impulse II pulled into the left hand lane and left the wheels turned to the left. The bridge abutment was coming at me fast. II shut my eyes, knowing it would soon be over. II felt II should have hit the bridge within seconds, but II hadn't. The car was slowing down, and as II opened my eyes it was moving from the left lane into the center of the highway. II pulled the car into the right lane and finally to the shoulder of the road, stopped, and turned the engine off. II remember looking out the windshield, and there before me was a field that II thought looked like wheat wafting in a breeze. More importantly, II felt an unexplainable peace. Never before had II felt so calm. What had happened? II felt changed somehow, yet physically it was still me.

As II sat there trying to take in what had just happened, II recalled that just before this happened II had heard the name, "Jacob". II remembered hearing people claim that God has touched them in a very special way and how II had doubted them. Had this happened to me? II can't say, but II believe something special happened that morning to bring me to my senses. Out of that experience came a belief that II had to seek the forgiveness of three people in my life. This wasn't something I had to do if II happened to get the chance. No, this was definite. II had to seek them out that day or the next. II had never experienced anything like this before. If it had been God talking to my spirit, II had been chastised severely. There on the side of the highway II bowed my head and prayed, acknowledging my wrongs, acknowledging what had happened, and asking God to take control of my life through His Son.

Later that afternoon as II returned home, II stopped on the other side of the highway by the bridge. As II stared across the highway, there was no field, only brush with dead leaves and brown weeds. After all, it was the month of March. What hadn't changed was the peace II felt and the necessity to make amends to the three people, one of whom was my wife. That night II explained to my wife what II had experienced and that II needed to ask forgiveness. II couldn't come right out and tell her about my secret identity. Instead II asked to be forgiven for the unfaithfulness in my life. She naturally assumed what most people would, that there was another female in my life. In a way she was right, but my fear and shame prevented me from explaining any of the details. II expected too much from her. My "true confessions" only placed more obstacles in our path.

For the next few weeks II didn't have to go into my closet. Perhaps it too was gone. II no longer seemed to feel the duplicitous spirit in me, but within weeks it was over. All those memories, all those feelings, and worst of all, all those desires and beliefs that II was still a female

47

hadn't disappeared.

We began our search for another church, one where the Bible was taught and believed. By attending a number of churches and asking questions we managed to find several churches in our city which met the criteria of being a Bible believing, Bible teaching church. For one reason or another we narrowed the list over a period of many months and ended up at the Baptist church where we had gone for counseling.

To become members of the church it was necessary for my wife and II to be baptized by immersion. Since both of us had been baptized as infants, we believed that we should now follow Christ through the waters of baptism to make a public declaration of our acceptance of Jesus as Lord of our lives. Following our baptism we were accepted into membership of the church and became part of the spiritual and social life of the church.

For a couple of years things began to improve in our relationship. The children had begun to make new friends through the youth activities, and the lessons we had learned at the seminar were ringing true. We had begun to take an active part in the ministry of the church. II became the Sunday School superintendent. My wife began speaking to women's groups in the province of how God was restoring our lives and family. Unfortunately, the children began to see the hypocrisy in our lives and the lives of other members of the church. Slowly the cracks were widening into gaps between them and the church family. One by one they began to drift away from the church for a while.

For myself, II continued suffering more and more the conviction of God about my life. All along my secret was still there. No amount of prayer, no amount of trying on my part gave relief or cure from the anguish II was feeling. II felt hopelessly inadequate before God. One Sunday morning II left the service, went to the office, and wrote out my resignation as the Sunday School Superintendent, placing it in the Chairman of the Deacons Board mail box without giving any reason for my action. II knew in my heart that if my secret were discovered II would bring shame to a whole church family as well as my own family. Better II be on the sidelines and stay in the shadows, away from people, where perhaps they wouldn't point so many fingers.

Life was returning to normal, whatever that meant. For me it meant hiding in my closet on a regular basis. What is normal for me might be totally unthinkable for you. When we use the term normal, what we are actually trying to say is, "The things that I know and find comfortable," and hiding in my closet had become what I knew, what was comfortable for me.

II was now under severe conviction that my thinking was far from what God had planned. The more II read and tried to understand what the Bible was saying to me, the more angry II became. As a result II became more and more depressed, more and more withdrawn, more

49

and more suicidal. It was an unending spiral into a dark bottomless pit. The further into the pit II fell the smaller the circle of light appeared at the top. There was a sense of hopelessness. II could see no possible way of climbing out. The more II spiraled the angrier II became at God. Was this some cruel joke? Had II confessed things to people and asked for forgiveness for nothing? What was the use? God really didn't care about me as a person any more.

No one else knew the anguish in my life. How could they? II had shut them out of my life and world.

4
Closet Living 101

By this time II had left the company where II had worked for so many years and was running my own little company out of the house. II did the selling, the designing, the assembly, the installation and the training.

Our company designed and installed computer systems for concrete plants to weigh the sand, stone, water and chemicals and put the mixture in the truck. It allowed the plants to type out a delivery slip for the driver and make a record of the shipment so that management could run the invoice program and update their accounts the next day.

Prior to beginning this business II had met a man who wrote a book entitled *God Owns My Business*. II was so impressed by this fellow that II had decided to follow his example. When II discussed this with the lawyer handling the incorporation, he thought II was nuts. In Canada it isn't possible to name God as the major shareholder of an incorporated company, so II decided that God would be my silent partner and made Him sales manager for the company.

When a sale was made, a sales commission was paid to God through a check sent to an evangelical church's missionary program in the city where the new system had been sold. The additional profits were used by our own church's benevolent fund to assist people in need in our community and the counseling ministry of our church.

II enjoyed the work II was doing, but for the family it meant that II was on the road traveling for great lengths of time. Concrete producing plants are relatively few and far between. This required me to chase after business from one end of the country to the other, so II decided to concentrate our business from Ontario to the Atlantic provinces, an area accessible by car when necessary. The company had the right product at the right time. It was the booming eighties. Business and construction were at all time highs. Finance and credit were abundant. Payment for our products was pretty well up front due to its custom nature. Risk was low and profit adequate to maintain a sound company.

My travel time in a year amounted to nearly five months, not all at one time, mind you, but when II left home it was usually for several weeks at a time. Each time II left II felt a sense of excitement and II dare say a feeling of release. For the next few weeks II had no one looking over my shoulder, no one asking where II was going, no one asking who was that on the phone. II was completely free to be me.

The first time II traveled stateside II was nervous to

pass through the U.S. Customs inspection at the airports. What if they questioned the contents of my luggage? How was II going to explain the two sets of wardrobes, one male and one female? As it turned out they never opened my luggage that time or any of the many other times II passed back and forth between the countries.

My female wardrobe seemed to increase every time II went away. It was a learning experience for me to find which labels came in which sizes and which ones came in my size. Female sizing is varied and ambiguous: S, M, L and XL mean different things in various stores and label lines. Then they really tried to confuse things when they introduced 1X and 2X sizing.

Needless to say II wasn't able to try the garments on in the store, so II devised a method of my own to determine if particular sizes were suitable. II carried two lengths of string in my wallet. One represented half the diameter of the top part of me, the other half the diameter of the waist. As II chose a garment, II secretly stretched the string across the garment to determine the fit. Soon II became adept at the labels and the sizing of each garment line and no longer needed the strings.

Personal grooming items were another trial and error shopping experience. II solved this through observation. II shopped with my eyes open. That is, II watched what women bought, their ages, and their appearance. II judged popular items by the stock levels on the shelves.

Fortunately hair growth on my body was a minor

problem. All my life II have had very little hair on my face and none on my body or legs, but there was one time II thought II could eliminate all traces of facial hair by using a hair remover. That evening II read the directions carefully, tested it on my arm as they suggested, and had no reaction. II felt safe to put it on my face for the pre-scribed length of time and then wash it off. The next morning as II entered the washroom II glanced at myself in the mirror expecting to see this hairless face. Instead II saw a face with a terrible rash. Everywhere II had applied the lotion to my face was red. How was II going to explain my face to a bunch of macho guys when II showed up at the concrete plant that morning? Truth is often stranger than fiction. They didn't believe me when II told them the truth of what II had done. Instead they offered me all sorts suggestions of what might have hap-pened. Perhaps II was allergic to the water or the soap at the motel, and so on. The redness didn't disappear quickly. It took several days before my face healed. The hair had gone and probably two layers of skin with it.

Another time on a trip to Granby II nearly didn't make it home. II had finished the revisions to a system on the Friday and decided to stay over until Monday to make sure the system was fully functional under maxi-mum operating conditions. When most plants got run-ning full tilt, a truck was loaded every three minutes, so when the computer system went down, production halted and panic took over. Each truck that failed to be loaded cost the producer eight hundred to a thousand dollars of lost product.

On the weekend II began to have severe heartburn and ate antacids like after dinner mints. Monday II felt okay. Everything at the plant was working as it should after a few minor adjustments. After dinner that evening II called home to let them know what flight II was taking the next day and when II would arrive at the airport, since they had offered to pick me up.

About midnight my heartburn returned with a vengeance, and it brought a companion, severe pains in my left elbow. For a while II thought II could ride the storm, but finally around two or three in the morning II knew II was in trouble when the elephant started sitting on my chest and wouldn't get off.

II decided II needed to get to the hospital, but as usual II had my other wardrobe to be concerned about. What if II died? Then people would find my secret. II had to dispose of everything. My room was on the third floor. II couldn't risk taking the elevator and having someone see me with this stuff on the way to the trash bins at the rear of the hotel. So II stole along the corridor and down the back stairs, being careful to prop the door open with my shoe while II disposed of the clothes in the dumpster. Then II went back into the hotel and along the first floor corridor to the front desk to ask the clerk for assistance to get to the hospital. All that extra exertion made the pain so intense that II was in a cold sweat by the time II reached the front lobby.

At the hospital they repeatedly gave me shots of morphine, until II finally lost consciousness. II came to at about ten oclock the next morning. As II focused my eyes, there standing beside me was the manager of the concrete plant. He was trying to comfort me by telling me not to worry, that he had made arrangements for everything. He had cleaned out my room and checked me out of the hotel, had made arrangements for my rental car to be turned in, and had requested that I be transferred to the Sherbrooke University Hospital coronary care unit.

Within a couple of hours II was whisked to the Sherbrooke hospital by ambulance, where II was scheduled for an angiogram and angioplasty if needed the next morning.

Meanwhile no one had thought to notify my wife where II was or what was taking place. She had gone to the airport that morning and waited and waited and finally given up and gone back home. Later that night, II think one of the nurses from the hospital called her to give her a status report on my condition. There wasn't much she could do. II was already in the best of all possible places, so she decided to join me in a couple of days and accompany me home on my return flight.

Two weeks after returning home she accompanied me on a trip to Nova Scotia to install another system. II appreciated her company on that trip, but at the same time II missed the opportunity to be my other self.

While traveling by myself II had many little mishaps and embarrassing moments cross-dressed as a female, only II didn't see it as being cross-dressed. II was simply dressing according to how II felt about myself. As II look back at my life, II sometimes think of myself as being a crossed-dressed female wearing traditional men's clothing. II know many people would find it hard to agree with this thinking, but II saw myself as a woman, and II wanted to be feminine.

There was a time in St. Johns, New Foundland during the winter when II dressed as a female to go out for dinner. The next morning II thought I'd simply slip next door to the fast food outlet for breakfast. II took off my gloves to retrieve the money from my pocket, and when II held it out to the girl behind the counter, oops, II suddenly realized II had not removed the nail polish from the night before. II felt a little silly sitting in the restaurant eating my breakfast with my gloves on.

Probably the most humiliating experience occurred in Dartmouth. II always tried to stay at a chain of motels where II could get a ground floor room with a sliding door leading directly to my car parked just outside the door. II generally unlocked this door as soon as II got in the room, and rather than smoke in the room II would often step outside. It also made it easier for me to exit my room as a female without going through the lobby.

One night II decided to go for a walk, and on my way out I picked up a package of cigarettes from the machine in the hall. Then II left by way of the side entrance to the motel. As soon as II had taken a few steps beyond the door, it closed and automatically locked behind me. With another step my feet went out from under me, and II found myself upside down in pain on the side walk. The cool night air had turned the mist from the harbor into ice. My hip, elbow and left side of my body ached.

Thankfully no one had seen me, II think. My skirt had flown up, my nylons were shredded, and my pride and head ached. Slowly II crawled back to the side of the building where hopefully II could grab hold of something and get to my feet. II felt for my keys, but they weren't in my coat pocket. I'd have to go to the sliding door. Slowly II made my way back to the screen door of my room. It was locked. Of all nights not to have left my sliding door unlocked. It meant the only way back into my room was to the clerk for the spare key to my room.

On another trip II almost disappeared. By this time in my life II knew for certain that the only thing II wanted was to be a complete female. In my closet was the haunting memory of that news report from Sweden, telling me that surgery could make it happen, but II didn't have a clue where to begin. II had heard that operations of this nature were happening in England. This particular time II was scheduled to fly out of Halifax for home. When II arrived at the airport, II parked my rental car in the regular lot, left a note in the driver's side visor, disposed of all my female wardrobe, and took my male clothes with me into the airport, leaving all my equipment locked in the trunk of the car.

As II walked into the airport, II passed the booth where II generally bought my wife a container of frozen lobster meat, but this time II wasn't buying lobster. II proceeded to the travel operator concession in the airport and purchased a non-refundable round trip ticket to England. There were a few hours before the connecting flight would take off for Montreal, so II went to the coffee shop.

As II sat there finishing my third cup of coffee, II felt consumed by guilt. My life was generally orderly, and this was perhaps the most irrational act II had ever conceived, simply to disappear and vanish with no explanations. II left the coffee shop and walked around the outside of the airport where people wouldn't hear me arguing with myself.

Finally II convinced myself to go for it. As II cleared security for the connecting flight, II was again confronted by my own rationality. When the boarding call came, II realized my legs had turned to jelly. II couldn't go through with it. The tears began to flow as II exited back through security, and once outside the airport II ran to the locked car where II could hide my brokeness.

By this time in my life II realized who II was and what was required to make me complete, but it didn't make life easier. II lacked commitment to myself, and II cared deeply for my family. The problem was that whenever

II looked at myself, II saw myself in a cracked mirror. There we were, him and her. For the next few years II was totally confused and angry, particularly at myself. If in fact II was a female in a male body, then II saw intimate relations with my wife as a lesbian relationship. If II allowed myself even to think of the possibility of being attracted to a male, then II would be gay. II began to realize my closet had another corner where II stored all those cliches about gays being molesters, demon possessed, and representing all the ills that beset humanity. II was extremely homophobic towards them without ever knowing one single gay or lesbian person. My homophobia was based solely on what II learned in the church. What made me fear the most was the possibility that II may be one of them.

My confusion about myself affected my marriage relationship in a very overt manner. II was afraid to feel intimate with my wife. As a result II shut down any feelings for anyone, fearing that II might be attracted to either gender. II didn't want to risk finding out that II was a homosexual, gay or lesbian, it didn't matter. II had enough to deal with in my gender issues.

II was uncomfortable sharing the same bed with my wife, and so to avoid these fears II often waited until she fell asleep, then I'd sneak downstairs and fall asleep in the easy chair with the T.V. on, pretending II had got up to watch the late show. There were many times when II sat in front of the boob-tube and II couldn't have told you what I was watching. II used to say it was my mind washer. It was another of my escapes. Often my wife would wake up and find me out of bed. Then from the top of the stairs I'd hear her voice reprimanding me for filling my head with all that garbage from the late night movies.

Finally II reached the point where II had abandoned my wife physically and emotionally. She constantly expressed her belief that my problems were due to some deep dark secret that was passed down to me as a result of the "sins of my father". What did she know that II didn't about my father's sins? Her comments only drove another wedge into our relationship. She was convinced that because he had been involved with the Masonic Lodge he had opened the family to satanic influences. This became a generalized explanation for everything. We were cursed to live under satanic rule. It explained my strange behaviors, the depression II and both of my sisters suffered, and anything else unexplainable.

By now II had reached a state of complete spiritual rebellion. II fired God as sales manager. II couldn't cope with the narrow mindedness of the puritanical fundamental church teaching. My wife had become so theological about every aspect of life that II began to see God through her as a vindictive punishing God. Everything contrary to her thinking had to be the result of satanic influences. II was angry and disillusioned at the thought of never being a satisfactory person and began drifting

61

away from worship. While II moved in this direction, she countered by moving in the opposite, embracing more and more of the church's rigid teaching, and the chasm widened between us.

Living a duplicitous lifestyle away from home was relatively easy. Living seven days a week at home was the problem. II couldn't be me. II had feelings of being incomplete when II wasn't dressed as a female. II started getting up at four or five o'clock every morning to spend the next couple of hours in my basement office. II could be completely alone except for Skip, our dog. He was up as soon he heard the stairs creek. As soon as II was in the office II changed into my female clothes. This went on for a couple of years. II didn't have to worry about anyone coming down, because II could hear when anyone upstairs started to move about, and II immediately went back into hiding. My confidence grew and so did my boldness. Eventually II began taking the dog for walks around the neighborhood dressed as a female and going into the garage for a smoke.

One morning in March as II returned from the garage after having a smoke, II heard a voice come from the family room as II passed by the door.

"What are you doing?"

My mind went into shock. My body froze in panic. All of a sudden II was enveloped in fear, shame, and humiliation. At first I hoped that she hadn't really seen me in my skirt, but II was silhouetted by the light on the stove. Of course she saw everything.

"What's going on? Why are you dressed like that?"

II couldn't squeeze a word out of my mouth.

"Come in here and sit down. II want to talk to you."

At that instant II felt like an animal caught in the beam of a flashlight. All II wanted to do was slither into a damp hole in the earth and never be seen again, but like a whipped dog, II sheepishly crawled into the family room and slumped into a chair facing my wife on the sofa.

"What do you think you're doing? How long has this been going on?"

She asked a million questions in rapid succession, but II had already retreated into my closet in my mind and shut the door, trying to shut out the sound of her voice.

Eventually she returned upstairs to get ready for work. II retreated to my office, hid my wardrobe and changed into male clothes. While she was upstairs, II gathered every medication II could find and swallowed it. II swallowed a real medicinal cocktail: pain killers (both prescription and over the counter), sleeping pills, heart medication, muscle relaxers, antibiotics. II went out and started her car, using the set of keys that II knew had no house key on the ring. II took all the pill containers down to the office. II would dispose of them later.

My wife was late and hurried out the front door. In her haste she turned to ask,

"Will you be okay?"

"Sure," II replied.

"We'll talk when II get home."

That's probably what II feared most. II knew what was going to be in store for that talk. We had talked on other subjects, but none was going to compare with this one coming up.

About half an hour later my son dropped by the house on his way to work. His mother had called him and asked if he would check in on me. After he left, II set about the task of removing all the evidence. While doing so II consumed a bottle of wine. My female clothing, the pill containers, and the wine bottle were disposed of in a garbage bag and taken out for the garbage collection that morning.

II drank a bottle of champagne that we had received as a gift at Christmas, because it was the only alcohol in the house, and II believed alcohol would speed up the reaction of the drugs in my system. II wanted my life to end quickly. It was working. Shortly II began feeling really strange. My head was swimming. II had cramps in the stomach. My mouth was dry. II couldn't keep my eyes open. II tried getting to the couch in the family room . . .

. . . the lights went out . . .

My wife returned home early that day, fearing that II might do something foolish. All of a sudden she realized she didn't have a key to the house. She rang the doorbell. She banged on the door. She knew II had to be in the house. Without a car II wouldn't walk a block. She managed to peer in through the sheer curtains II had drawn across the window. There II was, half on and half off the sofa, lying face down.

She ran to the neighbor's house, and with the aid of their daughter she managed to gain access to the house through the kitchen window and to call 911. The paramedics were baffled. II was comatose, my head was extremely swollen, and my blood pressure was dangerously low, but my pulse was strong. They couldn't determine what II had swallowed or how much. The garbage truck had already removed all the evidence as II had planned. However, when II arrived at the hospital, the emergency room staff began filling me with charcoal to try and absorb the drugs which had now been in my system for nearly five hours.

5
Closet Living 201

A few days later II woke up. II realized II wasn't in heaven. Nor was II in hell. But II was mad, mad as hell at God.

"Why can't you get out of my life?"

"Why can't II die?"

"What good am II to anyone?"

II remember mom coming to visit. We didn't talk much, but II had one question II wanted answered.

"Mom, why have II gone through life feeling II should have been a girl?"

An uneasy silence filled the cubicle in the intensive care ward, the only sounds coming from our breathing and the monitoring instruments.

"Well it's getting late," she said. "I'd better go."

Somehow II didn't expect I'd get an answer. Mom generally changed the subject when she didn't want to talk about something.

Once the doctors felt II was out of danger from what II had swallowed, II was moved to a ward on the fifth floor. Every fifteen minutes, round the clock, someone was checking on me. During the night II slept very little and only for brief periods of time. When the nurses came in to check, their flashlights played on the walls and ceiling like lightening bugs dancing to and fro. For five days II was kept on suicide watch. My mind was working overtime trying to figure out how II was going to finish what II had started. II didn't feel like II could face anyone. II simply wanted to die. II was convinced everyone in the hospital now knew II was queer. My family knew II was queer. II didn't feel II could withstand the barrage of hostile feelings now that people knew something terrible about me that only a few days ago had been my secret. All of our lives had been changed for ever.

II was on the floor where they put their psychiatric patients. Evidently that explained why II didn't have an identification band on my wrist or my name on the bed like the other guys in the ward, supposedly for confidentiality. II began to think of myself as a ghost. II was there, but II wasn't.

The first time II met the psychiatrist assigned to me, he greeted me as he walked from the door to my bed past the other three men in the room.

"So you're a cross-dresser," he announced to everyone present.

What a jerk! Couldn't he understand that II already hated myself. II had just attempted suicide to escape my pain and humiliation. II didn't have much self respect left, and he had just taken what little I had.

68

"It's common thing among men, you know."

Why couldn't he have waited till he got to my bed?

"So what's your problem? There's no harm in it. Enjoy yourself and get on with your life."

II tried to explain to him the religious and moral dilemma II found myself in, but he didn't share my religious beliefs, nor was he interested in that part of who II was.

As his visits went on, he tried to explain what a transvestite was, but II only became more upset. He told me that it was a common thing for men to dress in women's clothes, but the more he talked the angrier II got at myself and at him. Our sessions took place right there in the ward, within ear shot of the other three men. II feared what they thought of me.

"Why don't you join their club here in town? They go on regular shopping trips and have a night out on the town."

II didn't want to hear this crap. He wasn't saying anything that offered me any hope of restoring my life, just more of the same fear, anxiety and shame.

Each day when my wife came to visit, she insisted on knowing what the doctor and II had talked about. II couldn't begin to tell her about our discussions. Anything II might have been able to say was immediately swallowed up by my own shame. When she tried to discuss my case with the psychiatrist directly, the doctor shut her out. He simply refused to speak to her and avoided her when she went to his office in search of answers. She was completely excluded from my treatment beyond what II was willing to share with her myself. II learned that psychiatry is confidential. Family are excluded even though it may have a monumental impact upon their lives.

One day II noticed four young people opening the chart cupboards outside the door of each of the rooms and reading the hospital records for each of the patients in the rooms. When they were outside my room, II became very upset at what might be written in my records. II ran down to the nurses' station to complain to the doctor, but my concerns were merely brushed aside. After all, these were student nurses, II was told, working on an assignment. That's all well and fine, II thought, but what about my confidentiality? Even my own family were excluded from knowing anything, so why was it okay for students to be privy to sensitive information that might become public in a classroom discussion?

On one occasion the new senior pastor of our church came to visit. It was uncomfortable for both of us. II sensed he knew why II was in the hospital, since our brief talk centered on the absolute sin in my life and on my depraved mind. He told me the only way II could be healed was through confessing my sinful behavior to the church family and asking for their forgiveness. When II refused, he never visited me again.

Before II could be discharged II had to agree to at-

tend group and individual therapy sessions with the doctor who had been assigned to treat me. II didn't feel
comfortable with him, nor did II particularly like him or
his philosophy. II certainly would never think of trusting
him with my deepest secrets or of giving him the keys
that could unlock my closet. In order to get out of the
hospital II lied by agreeing to attend the sessions, which
II had no intention of doing.

After securing my release from the hospital II tried returning to the church services, but II felt uncomfortable.
II was uneasy. II was becoming paranoid around people.
What had they been told? What did they know? What
did they think of me? As people started to greet me,
II sensed by what they were asking that they thought II
had suffered a reoccurrence of my earlier heart problems,
but they all had different versions of the story. II became
fearful of blowing my family's well intentioned lies. Since
they weren't mine, II couldn't be sure who knew what
about me. II didn't feel comfortable talking to anyone,
so II left the services before they ended and sat in the
car hoping no one would see me there.

Neither my wife nor II had any confidence in the psychiatrist from the hospital, a feeling that perhaps had
some justification, since a couple of years later he was
charged with several counts of inappropriate sexual behavior with patients. My wife discussed our situation
with a doctor at our church to see if he could refer us to
a Christian psychiatrist. She was convinced that only a

Christian would have the keys to unlock my problem. As it happened, the doctor had a friend in another city who was Christian and a psychiatrist, but we needed to be referred by our family doctor. The family doctor refused to make this referral, believing that the doctor who had seen me at the hospital was competent and that there was no need to go outside the city. With the aid of two of our neighbors who were also doctors along with the doctor from the church, we changed to a new family doctor who made the referral to this Christian psychiatrist.

At the first meeting with this new psychiatrist my wife went into explicit detail of how she had found her husband cross-dressed as a woman that fateful morning.

"Well, what's the problem?"

"What's the problem?" she snapped back. "As a Christian, don't you see what's wrong with a man who wears women's clothes?"

"No, II don't see a major problem with transvestic fetishes," he assured her. "There's no known cure. It's non-fatal, and II suggest you allow your husband to pursue it at home."

While my wife and the doctor bandied back and forth on the spiritual implications, he had given me a sheet of paper with a group of questions. Each question had multiple answers weighted from 0 to 3. Called the Beck Test, it's one method of determining a person's depressive mood.

As II heard the two of them talking, II felt the longer

II took the less time they would have with me. When II finally handed the paper back to him and he assessed the score of my answers, he turned his focus to me.

"I'm concerned about your mood. You appear very depressed."

II wasn't overly startled by his assessment.

"How do you see yourself?"

"I'm a zero, a nothing. Everything II do or say is wrong or creates a problem."

"We need to begin working to bring your mood up." He handed me a prescription. "II want you to start taking these antidepressants today."

For weeks after that the routine was the same, and still my depression deepened, causing the doctor to increase the dosages of antidepressants until II had finally reached the maximum recommended dosage.

II don't think that any amount of antidepressant at that time could have removed my desire to die. Each week the doctor and my wife spent most of the session discussing the problems in the marriage from her point of view, with her ending up in tears.

At first II thought that the sessions were going to be about me and my cross-dressing, but II think the doctor dismissed that issue at the first session. What was significant to him was my suicidal tendencies and severe depression. He began trying to get to the root of the depression, and the doctor explained he was sensing a great deal of control on the part of my wife in our relationship. She no longer liked this doctor. He hadn't agreed with her on the cross-dressing issue, and now he was suggesting that she had some responsibility for my depressed state. II began to like this guy, finally someone who saw that II wasn't the total problem. Maybe he was someone II might be able to trust.

These were highly stressful months. II felt like II was being monitored by family members all the time, never being trusted out of their sight. The more stressed II became and the more anxiety II experienced, the more paranoid II became. In my mind everyone II saw knew all about me. They were talking about me, whispering about me behind my back. This one particular day II was driving the car in just such a state of mind. At a busy intersection II froze at the wheel in the middle of the intersection. Cars seemed to be coming at me from every direction at the same time. People were blowing their horns. II panicked, opened the door and ran in the direction of home, leaving the car running in the middle of the intersection.

The counselling sessions were hard for both my wife and II. It's not easy to work on a disintegrated relationship, especially when one person has a whole other secret side to their life. It wasn't easy for her simply to set aside her issues with the cross-dressing. II know it bothered her immensely. Sometimes the trips home became more intense than the time spent in the doctor's office.

Then the doctor started to do cognitive therapy using

the "Feeling Good" work book. Each visit we were given an assignment to work through individually and have ready for the next session for his assessment. One particular assignment involved a man whose life was caught up in deceit and lies. As II tried to work through this assignment, it seemed crazy for me to try and look through the mind of this fictional character. My life was the perfect subject. II began typing on my computer, and when II finished, II had my whole life experience in a chronological point form on four or five pages of paper. II hadn't really responded to the assignment questions, and for the life of me II have no idea why II suddenly chose to expose my dreams, my hopes, my feelings and my beliefs all in a neat orderly fashion.

Now my wife was much more fastidious about these assignments and often had her answers prepared well in advance. Then she would want to compare our answers. As we were about to leave that Tuesday, she asked if II had my answers with me and if II wanted to read hers? No, II didn't want her to see what II had written. II wanted to forget this week's assignment, but she insisted that II should take whatever II had prepared. Back down to the office II went and retrieved the answers from the computer, carefully rolling them up with an elastic band, making sure that on the first page there was a post-it note asking the doctor not to share any of this material with my wife or to discuss this material while my wife was present.

When we arrived at the doctor's, II did the Beck Test again, handed over my rolled up answers, and watched the doctor's face as he removed the elastic band, read the post-it note and flipped through the pages. Tears began to well up in my eyes, then the sniffles. By the time II had finished his test and handed it back to him, II was in a state of uncontrollable sobbing.

He slid my assignment answer sheet into the red file folder on his desk. He glanced at the Beck Test answers and swung around in his chair, picked up the phone and made a call.

"I wish to make an emergency admission this afternoon." Then he told them my name. "Yes. They'll be there in no more than thirty minutes." With his hand cupped over the mouth piece he turned to me. "I'm admitting you to Homewood. Now you can go voluntarily, or I can commit you. Which do you prefer?"

Voluntarily sounded less threatening than being committed. "Voluntarily," II answered.

"Yes, it's a form one admission," he said into the phone, and then he hung up. Turning to my wife, he said, "I've just admitted him to the Homewood for an indefinite period of time. They're expecting you shortly. Now I want you to go directly there when you leave here. Do you know how to get there?"

"No."

He gave us the directions, and we left, both of us in tears, not realizing how much our lives were about to change forever. II was terrified and confused. II was being sent to a mental hospital for an indefinite stay. Had my life sunk so low?

Finally after a few missed turns we ended up on the right street and pulled up in front of the main entrance of the hospital. We sat there for a few minutes, weeping, but neither of us was able to console the other. Just before we got out of the car II said to her, "II don't think I'll be coming home from here."

And then we walked through the front doors to the ward labeled Trillium, just inside the main doors to the left. It was locked. We pressed the buzzer and were greeted by a nurse who escorted us down a hallway to another locked door. She ushered us to the nurses' station inside the next set of locked doors. As II approached the door of the station, II noticed the banks of video monitors in front of the nurse.

He rose from his chair, bringing a blue plastic tray with him to the half door. "Please empty your pockets into this tray. Have you got a pen, comb, or anything else that's sharp or pointed? Please remove your belt and shoe laces. Have you any cigarettes, lighter, matches? Please put everything including your wallet into the tray. We'll keep them in here for you so they'll be safe."

The nurse then took us into the television room and what II guessed was the eating area. II couldn't help noticing the chairs chained to the floor, the table bolted to the floor, and the television enclosed behind a protective casing. The nurse explained that II was in a secure area because the doctor felt II was a serious risk to myself, and II was being placed under close surveillance for the next seventy-two hours. Then II was shown to my bed. It was in the surveillance room directly in front of the nurses' station with a window between the station and the room. My bed was directly in front of the window. The room had five beds in all. On one lay a woman, talking to herself. Another woman sat crouched on top of her bed. A man was sleeping on another.

After the nurse left us in the room, my wife and II went back into the TV room and sat there for a brief time. Nothing was said. No words could communicate the fears we both shared. As she left, she hugged me and said, "Perhaps now you'll get the help you need."

II watched as she waited at the door for the nurse to release the lock. She walked down the hall and around the corner and out of sight. On the way to my room the nurse gave me a couple of pills to settle me down. Was it that obvious? Men don't cry.

As II lay on the bed the tears flowed. II was scared. Maybe this was where II would spend my life. Everything looked so bleak. The surroundings were austere, heavy expanded metal screens on windows that wouldn't open more than two inches, no mirrors, no doors, cameras everywhere. The pills were taking affect as II lay there in the fetal position. My eyes were getting heavy with tears and sleep.

When they woke me for supper that evening II had no appetite for grilled liver and green beans. Every hour seemed to take ten to pass. Seventy-two hours would be an eternity. II didn't want to go to the bathroom. There was no privacy. There were no doors. What had happened to me as a person?

Part III

Hi, God.
Do You
Know II'm
Hurting?

6
II'm Out

II was terrified and paranoid of the other people in the ward. II wanted to sleep, but my mind raced, thinking all sorts of dreadful things that were going to happen to me in there. Later in the evening a young female nurse came to give me my medications and sensed the terrible state II was in. She had a soft comforting voice, not at all like the male nurse during the day, who appeared gruff and was ho-hum about it all.

She took me into the TV room where we sat on one of those benches chained to the floor. She put her arm around my shoulder in an effort to calm me. II sniffled to push back the tears that filled my eyes and were already gently rolling down my cheeks.

Without any sort of warning every one of my defensive walls crashed to the floor. II barely whispered. "It's like there are two people inside me. The one is so dominant that II've lost control."

"It's okay. Just let go."

There was silence, with neither of us saying a word. II buried my face in my hands and doubled over to hide my fear and shame. "II feel like a female," II said, and then the tears flowed.

For the first time in my life II had told someone who and what II was all about. Perhaps the earth could now open up and swallow me. There was release coupled with fear. My mouth was dry, my eyes filled, and my stomach felt like it was in knots. She put her hand in mine and gave it a little squeeze, as much to say that she cared and understood. We sat there for a long time before II returned to my room and finally drifted off to sleep.

When II awoke in the morning every fear II ever had was there to haunt me plus some new ones. Words spoken are like the wind. Once out they can't be gathered back. But there was also a great feeling of relief and a small sense of freedom.

Soon my term in observation ended, and II was moved to the general ward, where II had more freedom to move about and have a smoke. On the main ward II was assigned a prime nurse who would look after my treatment, a doctor who would try and help me deal with the stresses in my life, and a social worker who would help me adjust to becoming a consumer survivor, an ex-patient of a psych hospital. These people over the next many weeks became very helpful in moving my self-esteem one step at a time from a zero to a one on a scale of a hundred.

II wish the experience for my family could have been as positive. Unfortunately they couldn't let go of the dreams and the expectations they held for my life.

As the days went by and II demonstrated that II could be trusted not to bring harm to myself or anyone else, II was allowed more and more privileges. The staff admitted that they had no experience with persons with a gender identity dysfunction, so they made arrangements for my use of the doctor's reference library where II could spend my time researching my problem. II desperately wanted to find a cure.

Weeks went by, and nothing II read indicated a cure was possible. II didn't want to tell the family my secret just yet, and of course the staff wouldn't discuss my case with them, so they remained in the dark until II was ready to make the move.

My depression hadn't been cured, but my mood had elevated from the critical level where it had been when II first arrived. The thought of suicide was still an option of last resort, but II would never admit to it for fear of being placed back in the locked ward or losing my privileges to go to the library and the dining room for my meals.

Finally the family were pressing me for answers, and since II was feeling more comfortable talking to the staff about my innermost feelings, the time was coming when II felt safe to express myself. One sunny afternoon my wife came to visit. We went for a little walk around the grounds and finally sat on a bench overlooking the gardens. II wasn't going to bring up the subject, but then she asked, "Do they know what the problem is yet?"

"They call it a gender identity dysfunction. The long

and the short of it is, II'm a trans-sexual."

"Impossible. You're a man."

"Well, yes and no. You only know the outside. Inside II see a woman."

"This is all because of wrong thinking. You've allowed Satan to control your thinking."

After she left that day, my mood level dropped several points, and II spent a lot of time just laying on the bed in a state of depression. She was now inside my closet, and one word described everything about me. "Trans-sexual" said it all.

A few days later when the kids came to visit, we again went to that same spot, and II told them what II had told their mother. II tried to reassure them that II loved them very much, that no matter what was to happen in the future II would always be their father.

We were all frightened and unsure of what this meant. Each member of the family had our own separate unspeakable beliefs, emotions, fears and expectations, and over the next several weeks these began to emerge. There was shock, disbelief, anger, betrayal, loss, broken dreams and promises, the effective death of whatever it is that they held to be true about me. II felt a sense of mourning, similar to a physical death, as the family began to express their emotions.

The hospital staff tried to bridge the gap they saw opening between us by arranging a family conference involving the professional staff, the family and me. It was

86

to be our chance to learn the hell in each of our lives and to develop effective ways to cope with it. Unfortunately this conference didn't have the affect they had hoped. During the session very little was asked or expressed by the family, and so they really didn't take advantage of the professional advice. When the staff concluded and had left the session, the true emotions came out. At this point II was still mentally fragile, and the least little upset sent me into a depressed suicidal state. Following this session II was again heavily drugged and spent the next several days in my room on the bed in a fetal position wishing II was dead because II felt so guilty for their feelings.

They continued to visit and began seeking a cure for me. II too was looking for that cure, but II think we were looking in different directions. As a person accustomed to computers and data storage II felt that if my problem was a result of wrong beliefs or wrong thinking or wrong memories, then just like a computer it should be possible to zap my brain and remove this wrong stuff. II discussed the possibility of shock treatments, radical brain surgery or whatever else might be possible. The psychiatrists were in agreement. There were no treatments that would "fix" my problem short of death or a sex change. After all, the human mind is not a computer, and you cannot edit the history recorded there.

The family held the premise that my problem was spiritual in origin, the result of wrong thinking and actions, or even the "sins of my father". They sought counsel from the Christian community, who knew little or nothing about gender identity dysfunction and simply confirmed everything the family believed and wanted to hear, even to the point of suggesting that II was demon possessed and needed to be exorcized. II was told that II was a reprobate trans-sexual bent on my own destruction and the ruination of the family.

From my readings in the medical reference books of the hospital library II found no evidence that would dispute the doctors, nor did II find the slightest hope for a cure. Cures are for illnesses. Gender identity dysfunction is not a sickness. Even though my depression was a physical illness, it could not be cured, only controlled through drugs. However, there were no drugs to control gender identity.

All my life II tried to control my thinking. II tried desperately and inflicted a lot of mental pain and degradation on myself, but II couldn't help knowing who II was. That person lived inside me every hour of the day.

Fortunately most people never have to stop and think about their gender identity. They never have to ask themselves the question, "Am I a boy or girl?" Most people just automatically know who they are and live their lives accordingly. However, trans-sexuals battle with this confusion from very early in their lives, and the question never leaves their minds. Outwardly they see one gender. Inwardly they feel like they belong to the other. It's so difficult to put into words the confused emotions and the overwhelming desire to be the other gender we believe we are, to be able to convey the conundrum we find ourselves forced to live, usually in secret, because of the fear of rejection and of being ostracized by society. If it were possible to change that aspect of me, II simply wouldn't be me.

Gender identity isn't a thought process. It isn't a whim. It has nothing to do with evil spirits. It's the very foundation of my being. It's my very existence, and it's based on whether II see myself as male or female. In non-medical terms, it's brain sex. It's the combination of every aspect and experience of my life. It's who II am.

The staff believed that my depression was becoming controlled, but before they were prepared to discharge me they needed to be assured II was mentally able to withstand the tests and trials outside the institution, so II was allowed to go home for a trial period of two days. My prime nurse encouraged me to utilize the skills II had developed in my career designing software solutions for complex problems and decision making. She showed me how to use my strengths instead of my weaknesses.

Basically computers are very dumb machines, just like the wall switch that turns the lights on or off. They can only make two decisions, on or off, yes or no. What they have is the amazing capacity to make many of these decisions in a very small amount of time. Unlike the human mind, they dont have an indeterminate state or a maybe state. A computer therefore analyses a mountain of these on/off states and produces a result that is translated into an action one way or another. When we try to do the same thing mentally, sometimes a maybe, a doubt, forces us into a state of inaction with dire consequences. For me this state was procrastination.

All decisions can be logically charted, showing actions and questions which can be answered yes or no. Succeeding actions and questions result from either one or the other paths in response to the answer to each question. An entrepreneur makes a decision to start a business in much the same fashion. First he asks, "Do II want to start this business?" Assuming his answer is yes, his next question is, "Will it be successful?" At this point he looks at all the data he has assembled about the business, and his decision is yes or no. Every other decision he makes will involve the same process. There is no provision for maybes, no room for indecision.

This is the process my nurse and II worked through concerning my two day home trial. How was II going to respond when certain events took place? What outcome was II looking for and expecting? II needed to be clear about what II considered safe conditions for all concerned but especially for myself so II wouldn't lapse into despondency and suicidal thoughts or actions.

After II had committed this process to paper so they could review and evaluate my decisions, they gave me my two day pass. II was looking forward with a certain

90

apprehension to the opportunity to be back in a family setting after so many weeks in an institution. My wife picked me up that evening and took me home. She had prepared one of her great roast beef dinners with pan roasted vegetables and gravy. What a treat.

After supper we took our tea into the family room for what II anticipated would be a relaxing evening. Wrong. My wife began almost immediately to express the anger, fear, frustration and doubts that she had suppressed over the past several weeks. II tried to listen to what she was saying and to be sensitive to her need to express these things, but there were those tiny phrases she would include in discussion, phrases that cut to the bone. Almost immediately my mind focused on my decision chart. II no longer felt mentally safe. Sensing the accuracy of the possible scenarios in the chart, my decisions became almost instinctive. As II have said before, II feared confrontations. II feared discussions with my wife because II always felt inadequate, and when provoked she had a sharp skill with words that cut me to pieces. II noticed the phrases II had heard so often and hated, "childish", "immature", "you never", "you always" dominated the discussion very quickly, and it was fast becoming a rout.

"Stop, please stop, I'm not ready for this yet. Can't we just be together without this confrontation?"

"You're going to sit there and take it like a man."

"This isn't going to work. II need to go back to the hospital. II can't stay any longer. Mentally II don't feel safe."

"No! I'm not taking you back tonight."

II tried to tune out and turn off, but II couldn't. My mind had gone into an indecisive state. How much simpler it would be if our decision making capacity were as definitive as a computer. Within a fraction of a second my mind had processed the chart of decisions, and II knew instinctively what II must do.

Angrily II rose from the chair to take my empty cup to the kitchen sink. II was no longer in that indecisive state. II paused in front of her. "If this is how we're going to react to one another every time we're together, then we're going to separate. There's no point being together. We've hurt one another enough." For the first time in my life II had stated in no uncertain terms just how II felt. II had made a difficult decision without waiting for someone else to do it.

When II reached the kitchen counter, there lay the large butcher knife II had used to carve the roast. An instantaneous thought flashed like lightening through my mind, "Go ahead pick it up," but what was II going to do with it, use it on me or her. This scenario wasn't on my chart. II reeled from the sink and the knife and literally ran out the front door, with the wooden screen door banging closed behind me. II began walking, consumed by anger and rage. II had never experienced the emotion of rage in my life, but II did that night. II can now see how in that state of mind anything is liable to happen, and luckily for us it didn't happen that night.

We lived on the edge of town, and shortly II found myself walking along the rural road on the west side of the river, not really thinking about where II was going. When II came to the bridge that led to the highway, II decided to jump off the bridge into the river and the rocks below.

As II reached the center of the bridge, a car came along slowly over the bridge, so II just kept walking to the end of the bridge and the highway on the east side of the river. II came to a little fresh water spring where people often came to fill their water bottles. II stopped for a sip and realized II was headed in a direction that held no promise of help. II turned and started walking back into town along the highway and then along the foot path that had been constructed out of the abandoned railway tracks. When II reached town, II stopped at a coffee shop to gather my thoughts. II had $2.20 in my pocket. II could afford a coffee.

As II drank the coffee II thought of my son who lived a few blocks away on top of the hill. When II was finished, II headed off in his direction, but when II arrived, his house was in darkness. II had no idea of the time, but II knocked on the door anyway. There was no answer, so II continued walking with no preconceived destination in mind. II needed to escape, and II knew that home was not a safe option this time.

II had been walking now for hours, and eventually

II passed the police station wearing only shorts, a short sleeved shirt and a wrist band from the hospital in the rather chilly night air. Several police cars passed me but none stopped. II continued walking, wondering if they might notice the wrist band and stop to question me. II had now reached the opposite side of the city. Subconsciously II guess II was heading back to the only place of safety II had, the hospital.

II decided to have another coffee before II set out on the walk through the rest of the night and back to the hospital. Spending that last $1.10 on a coffee somehow symbolized my entire worldly poverty. II realized there on the bridge on the outskirts of town that II wouldn't be going home from the hospital, and that was okay.

As II left town that night, II said goodbye to my city, my family, my church, my career, my business, my worldly possessions. There was nothing there to hold me anymore. II was no longer the person they thought II was, and II could no longer be the person they wanted me to be. II cried. II swore. II sang. II prayed. With each aching step there was a release, a sense of empowerment and control over my life, feelings II had never allowed into my life.

Nine hours after II had left the house, II arrived at the locked front doors of the hospital in the early hours of the morning. The sun of the new day gave a glow to the sky as II rang the buzzer to summon the security staff. The nursing staff had been waiting for me. The family had notified them that II had gone missing the night before, and they had searched in vain.

At first II feared being put back in the locked ward, but instead they made me a cup of coffee, allowed me to have a shower and change my clothes. II had just walked nearly fifty kilometers. My hands were swollen. II hadn't realized that hands could swell from being swung while walking for a long period of time. They actually ached from the swelling. The stones along the shoulder of the road had cut through the thin foam rubber soles of my shoes, shredding my light cotton socks, cutting my feet open, imbedding pieces of the cotton into the cuts. II was tired and sore, but II knew II was in a safe place.

The next few days II began working with the social worker, preparing a resume so II could start the process of job hunting. We defined my experiences and the business skills II possessed. II was given privileges to leave the grounds in search of work, to deliver resumes. Unfortunately II was a has been at the ripe age of 55, with the reply address and phone number of the Health Center.

People II spoke to were polite but uninterested. II had heard of the stigma of mental illness. Now II was experiencing it. Financially II was broke. II couldn't even afford to wash my clothes in the laundromat at the Health Center. That's when the social worker stepped in and obtained a personal care allowance from Social Services.

She continued working with me in the search for work

and at the same time began helping me look for a place to live when II was discharged. II never realized how difficult it was to be homeless by choice. Social assistance is a great help for a person attempting to begin life over again, but unfortunately their help doesn't overcome society's view of you as a non-person. II began to understand the fear that women have to leave abusive homes. How do they begin anew? Who's there to help them start fresh? They are non-persons, no credit, no income, no fixed address except the shelter, and no telephone where they can be reached. Who wants to hire or rent to non-persons? We have become a society of people identified by a long list of numbers. If you don't believe me, try ordering a pizza – "Telephone Number Please." Try making a return to a major department store – "Postal Code please." Without these, you've become a non-person.

The hospital staff were now concentrating on therapy for my release. II was allowed to make contact with the psychiatrist who had sent me to the hospital so that upon my release there would be follow up treatment. When II expressed my concern to him that II was being released shortly and II had not been able to find work or a place to live, he offered to assist me. At our next meeting he explained to me that his friend managed a conference center at the Jesuit grounds just north of the city. II could stay there until II found a suitable place to live. Besides having a place to stay, II would also have priest there who was willing to help me with the spiritual concerns that were troubling me.

II had stuffed lots of misguided ideas and beliefs in my closet. They hung there like smelly old clothing that couldn't easily be parted with. One of those old beliefs concerned Catholicism. II was a Baptist. II believed we had the right answers to salvation, and they didn't. As II look back now, God had a special purpose for bringing this priest into my life, if for no other reason but to rid me of my arrogance

The day had come. The staff at the hospital were confident that they had done everything possible to ensure that my depression and suicidal thoughts were under control. Before my release from the hospital the doctor sent an application to the Gender Clinic of the Clarke Institute in Toronto requesting an appointment for me to be evaluated. They were the only specialists in Ontario qualified to diagnose and treat trans-sexuality. My outside psychiatrist would work with me to address my gender issues and monitor my depression over the coming months.

Moving day from the hospital came, and II felt apprehensive. II was nervous about leaving the comfort and safety of the hospital. II was a baby bird being kicked to the edge of the nest to see if II could really fly now that II had faced my greatest fear.

7
II'm Scared

II arrived at the Jesuit conference center that afternoon
and was met by Father John, the priest who was friends
with my doctor. He didn't know anything about me,
except that II was in need of a place to live for a short
period of time and that II didn't have any money. Father
John became a close friend of mine over the next few
weeks, and II felt comfortable confiding in him about my
gender identity problems. II wanted to be on the up and
up with him, just in case something came back to haunt
us because II hadn't been completely open.

The conference center is located in the building once
used as the residence for novice priests. My room was
one of the "cells" (rooms) on the third floor, measuring
seven feet by ten feet with very sparse furnishings, a bed,
a chair, a desk, a lamp, a wash basin and a cupboard that
had been used for their clothes.

When II left the hospital my worldly possessions didn't
fill a supermarket plastic grocery bag. All of my possessions had been left behind at home. That night II laid
there in the dark listening to the old building talk. It's

moans and groans echoed the story of a well used building. Sounds came from every direction. If only II'd been able to interpret the stories being told. I'm sure it would have been a great story to hear the antics of those young priests, their laughter, their prayers, and yes, even their doubts. How II wished there was someone to talk to. II'd have settled for the intrusion of a nurse shining her flashlight in the door.

In the mornings II walked back into town to make my rounds looking for work and dropping off resumes. Around noon hour II always tried to make it back to the downtown area so II could go to the drop-in center, where for a dollar II could get my meal for the day. In the afternoon II checked the want ads of the free papers at the drop-in, looking for a place to live. The lower cost apartments were hardly habitable even for the cockroaches dwelling there. Each time II walked into town II passed a building II believed must be condominiums because it was so well kept. II promised myself someday II would be back on my feet and live in a place like that.

Eventually II responded to an add in the paper for an apartment advertised as a seniors building. When II arrived at the address that the lady had given on the phone, II realized it was this building II thought was a condominium. The apartment had everything II imagined would suit my needs and more. It was much larger than anything II had seen, and the cost was only slightly more than the sub-standard places. II said I'd take it immediately without considering how II was going to pay for it. In the office II had to fill out a questionnaire. The same questions that had tripped me up in the past came up, present address, income, references.

II had promised myself to be truthful in all my dealings, but when II had done so at other apartments II had been turned down because II had no fixed address and no telephone. II wasn't going to lose this opportunity to acquire a decent place to live. II felt my self-esteem was worth the risk. II gave my address as that prior to the hospital, my income from the previous year, and the phone number of the conference grounds. II explained that II had separated from my wife and was staying at the conference grounds because II needed to settle some personal spiritual concerns.

II had come to an agreement with Father John where II could work for my room and board by helping around the conference center while II was there. He and II had developed a friendship, and II continued to help out long after II had moved into the apartment. II had something to keep me busy and another friend to talk with.

The social worker came to visit one day and was pleased that the Jesuits had taken me in for a short duration. II explained that II hadn't been successful yet in finding a job, but that II had located an apartment and what the cost would be. She took down the particulars and said she'd be back the next day. She kept her word. She came back with news that all the arrangements were made. They were raising my monthly allowance and were including a relocation allowance to cover the deposit.

My mom and sisters helped me move into the apartment by providing some used furniture and household necessities. The Jesuit community also helped out with some furnishings to get me started. II thought, "How blessed can a person be?"

As II look back over those days, II see a God true to his covenant with me that He wouldn't leave me or forsake me. It's completely the opposite of what II've done. II've abandoned friends when II've had enough of their nonsense. Even though II had fired Him from my company and had became angry with Him because II couldn't die, He continued to stay beside me. Since those days II'm able to appreciate the people who crossed my path, the assistance II received, the spiritual and psychological guidance that was offered to me. It was merely a foretaste of what was to come.

My physical needs were now looked after. II had a place to call home, a place where II was safe from the family. Now II had to attend to the rest of me. Who was II? Who did II want to be? How was II going to achieve my aspirations?

There was another corner in my closet that held all my biases. One was specifically for loafers, those who lived off the backs of others, welfare recipients, people too lazy too work. After all, II had always earned everything my family enjoyed. Why should II be required to support people who were just too darn lazy to get out there and make it on their own the way I did? I was pretty self-righteous about my giving and intolerant about those who did the taking. My life had to be brought to the point of complete bankruptcy before I was willing to change my perspective.

Suddenly my life was in that corner of the closet. I began to see that sometimes life's circumstances aren't on a level playing field. Not everyone had received the opportunities that I had. It's frightening for me now to think that had it not been for a great many gracious people who were willing to share their resources, I might not be writing this story. For a long time I ate in a drop-in center where food and operating costs had been donated. I received left over food from the conference center. My furnishings were donated to me. I obtained used clothing through charity outlets. I picked through garbage to find useable items. The proud are often brought low, and I've been on my belly, so hopefully that area of the closet is cleaned out.

The next twelve months of my life were a living nightmare.

I remember that as children we used to walk along the railroad tracks, trying to keep our balance on the rail. Sometimes we had two feet on the rail, then one foot slid to the ties, then we'd get two feet back up on the rail. When we got tired of sliding off the rail, we'd sort of hop along with one foot up and one foot down on the tie, alternating from one side of the rail to the other. That's how my life went during those twelve months after releasing my secret identity, unsteady, unsure, flip flopping, trying to maintain an even footing, but failing in every step along the way.

Father John became a very dear friend. At first II wasn't sure how a literal interpreting fundamental Baptist and a Roman Catholic were ever going to see eye to eye on anything. II was right. We didn't. But he had a lot to teach me about how II saw myself in God's creation. He showed me why God didn't use cookie cutters when he made us. He taught me how to look at the scriptures in a different way. He gave me new insights into prayer. He asked questions that sent me searching for my own answers. He believed there were no wrong answers. God would only give me as much as II could understand. As we continued to talk, another question might cause me to search and build on what God had already shown me. Our relationship wasn't a teacher-student relationship. Rather, he was a guide into a searching process. He never once gave me a straight forward dogmatic answer to any question II asked. This upset me tremendously at first, because II couldn't get immediate gratification. II had grown accustomed to pat simplistic answers to spiritual questions.

As a literal fundamentalist Christian II saw everything spiritual as black and white, right and wrong, do and don't, two states. Just like a computer, II had been mentally programmed to accept without question the teaching of others, which left no room for the Holy Spirit to work with me as an individual.

In the following months there developed an awakening of my spirit. The Jesuits' excellent reference library was made available so II could spend as much time as II needed searching through various translations of the Bible, reading commentary after commentary, looking for explanations of scripture passages, reading historical accounts to better grasp an understanding of the people and times when the Bible was written, how it had been passed down through the centuries, how the English language had changed through the years, how meanings of words had changed.

It was the most beautiful time of the year, my favorite season, autumn: the earthy smell of dead leaves, the sweet smell of apples rotting on the ground in the orchard of the grounds, the color of trees decked in royal reds and yellows, the coolness of morning dews, the warmth of afternoon sun and the freshness of the evening air.

Father John once asked me, "What do you hear God saying to you when you pray?"

"II guess II've never heard Him tell me anything."

"Why is that?" He continued to probe.

"II guess II'm too busy telling him where II hurt and asking for what II need," II replied.

"Then how do you know if He's listening to you?"

"II guess if my prayer gets answered or not."

105

"So if you don't get what you've asked for then He's not listening, according to you."

"Something like that," II replied.

"What do you think prayer is?" he asked.

"Communication with God."

"You and II communicate, so what's happening when we do?"

As the night wore on II thought, "This guy's getting on my nerves. Never a direct statement or answer, just question after question. II need straight forward answers to my tough questions."

"Communication is ten percent talk and ninety percent listening," he said. "I think you need to learn some communication skills, especially with God, before you're going to find many of the answers you're looking for. Here's an exercise I'd like you to try. For the next seven days I want you to go outside and sit in various places around the grounds for the afternoon, rain or shine. Then I want you to close your eyes while you sit and visualize sitting on a bank along a river. Visualize a man walking towards you. He stops. It's Jesus. He sits down beside you. Then we'll get together in a week or so."

When we got together again, II thought he was going to ask me what II had learned from the exercise.

"When you were sitting there," he asked, "did you see yourself as a man or a woman?"

II paused in surprise. "A woman. II was a woman talking to the Lord."

106

"You see, God doesn't discriminate against you the way you discriminate against yourself. He didn't walk by you because you see yourself different from the way others see you. The important thing is, did the two of you communicate while you sat there?"

Sheepishly II had to admit, "Yes. There were periods when II stopped talking and listened, but there were many more times when II swear God was out on the golf course because it seemed like a great waste of time."

That experience was the first time II ever remember having a conversation with God. You know, sometimes we have friends and family who never listen to what we have to say. When they do that to me II'm irritated beyond measure. That was what II had been doing when II prayed. II never allowed God to add anything to the conversation.

Another evening Father John and II were having a cup of coffee together in his office, and as he bent forward to take a sip through his straw, he paused and cocked his head in my direction.

"You know, I'd hate to be your neighbor."

He shot that one at me straight from the hip. II never saw it coming. II can't even remember what we were discussing that night, but that comment, seemingly from nowhere, shot like a rubber band past my face, narrowly missing my nose. My reply was indignant. "Excuse me!"

"I'd hate to be your neighbor," he repeated.

"Why?"

107

"You need to answer that question for yourself."

You know, it took a couple of weeks before II could even come close to finding the reason he didn't want to be my neighbor.

When II began with a concordance looking into the word "neighbor", II came upon a passage where Jesus is speaking to a group of the Pharisees.

As II read this passage, II could visualize myself in that group of self righteous men. Of course II knew who my neighbors were, but that isn't what Jesus was communicating. II had missed the whole point of Jesus' words. II had already demonstrated how II loved God. II fired Him from my company. All my life II had heard this passage recited, but II had never paid much attention to the deeper meaning behind it.

Father John had detected my anger and self loathing not only from what II said but also from my body language. After all, II had already told the psychiatrist II considered myself a zero and a nothing. Why would II see anyone else differently? II guess until II could begin to love myself there was little hope for me to renew or even establish a love for God, or anyone else for that matter.

Loving myself wasn't an overnight success. It's not like you say to yourself, "Well, tomorrow morning I'm getting up and loving myself," and bang, it's accomplished. II'm still struggling with it, hopefully progressively. II'm afraid its going to take a lifetime.

Father John's astute observation and the Spirit's prodding in this area of my life were major stepping stones, corner stones perhaps, in a new foundation that has supported me ever since, allowing me to become the person II am.

While all these spiritual things were taking place in my life, II still had to deal with my family and their pain. Some weekends II went back home to see if we could find common ground to accommodate one another's needs. Weekend after weekend we tried. Each weekend feelings were stepped on, hurtful remarks made, accusations hurled. Compromise was my responsibility alone. It was necessary for me to be a man visually and actively just like they had always thought II was.

II was also dealing with my depression, some brought on from the stress of living two lives, some from being found out, some from family predisposition, some because of the guilt II felt for putting my family through this. II was bounced around like a yo-yo, sometimes sleeping for days on end, or not sleeping at all, or not eating for days, or overeating, or just sitting in a mental vacuum. In my closet II often practiced 'stinken thinken', imagining how much better everyone would be if II were dead, developing a fool proof method for my next suicide attempt, determined there would be no more failures.

Then II would be back in the spiritual realm seeking answers from God, only to have my family criticize my attempts at seeking counsel with a Catholic priest and a

Christian Psychiatrist, neither of whom they considered to be Christian. They believed neither of them had any message except from the devil.

Have you ever been faced with the statement, "It's our way or the highway"?

That was my predicament. Any compromise in restoring relationships was strictly my responsibility. II had to go back in the closet and essentially deny who II was. Some asked me to take part in an exorcism of my soul to cast out the evil spirits they said II had permitted to take up residence in my mind. Another required me to attend meetings with a Christian based group called "New Visions". They were affiliated with Exodus, a well known and controversial "save the gays" group in the United States, and they claimed that their Christian based counseling had rescued gays, lesbians and trans-sexuals from lives of degradation. The meetings were held in a secret location in Kitchener. The group II attended was comprised of the leader and two gay men. When II questioned the group about their success, the leader had to admit he knew of no one who had left the gay life. He had no experience with trans-sexuals and neither had any of his colleagues. As far as his own conversion, he openly admitted that he was still gay, but that he had chosen to live a heterosexual life by marrying and having children and that he satisfied his gay feelings through masturbation and gay fantasy. Of the other two, one was trying to be celibate, and the other simply satisfying his gay feelings through masturbation. Three meetings were all II needed to determine there was no help for me there. They believed that masturbation and gay fantasy were acceptable as long as it didn't involve lust towards another gay person.

All this was happening within the first few months of my release from the hospital, and II still had not been scheduled appointments with the Clarke Institute Gender Clinic. Out of sheer desperation to find assistance II telephoned the Clinic on two occasions trying to find help. II asked if there were support groups. Was there anyone in the area going through the same things II was trying to cope with? No, they said there was no help they could offer, and no, there was no schedule yet for my referral to the clinic. The only advice they offered was, "You'll have to cope the best you can on your own."

Shortly after taking up residence in my apartment II was invited to attend a meeting for psychiatric survivors. The group in town was one of thirty-two similar groups around the province sponsored by the Ontario Ministry of Health. It was the government's attempt to replace the mental health care traditionally supplied by institutions by allowing patients to become peer support for one another. With a budget of three and a half million dollars the government believed it could cut costs and still support people suffering from mental illness and patients discharged from mental hospital facilities.

Along with a couple of friends II had met in Homewood, II decided it might provide some social contact without a lot of cost, so why not go and at least see what they offered. Some of the groups in the province had developed successful organizations. However, our local group was fraught with disorganization, in-fighting and power struggles. The first few weeks we attended didn't seem too bad, but as the weeks went by, we began to see lack of leadership, controlling personalities, preoccupation with mistreatment by hospital staff and doctors, and obsession with drugs. One person's symptoms soon became the symptoms of the group. II became wound up in this organization when they asked me to sit on the board of directors because most of the others had resigned over one dispute or the other. At one of the previous board meetings the police were required to break up the meeting when it turned violent between the directors.

The fall and winter months that year were turbulent periods with not much being resolved. II felt like II was in a holding pattern, unable to resolve my gender identity to my satisfaction. In the midst of all this turmoil the house II had owned with my wife was sold. This meant more involvement on my part with the family, which II didn't particularly relish due to my feelings of guilt for causing the hurt they had to experience. II believed it was my responsibility, however, to provide for my wife in the best way II could, and that meant allowing her to retain the car, the house, and all its contents. II didn't feel that her standard of living should suffer because II had decided that II could no longer live in secret. After all, she was not responsible for the catastrophe this gender thing was causing in her life.

Before she could make an offer to purchase a smaller home, however, her lawyer required that II provide documentation to release the proceeds of the sale to her. II approached two local lawyers who refused to draw up such a document, fearing that II would later regret my decision and turn around and sue them for bad advice. II sent my wife's lawyer a letter stating that II was relinquishing the proceeds of the sale to her. He knew about our separation but had been led to believe that my stay in the mental hospital was the cause of the separation. He was uneasy with my decision and requested a letter from my psychiatrist stating that II was of sound mind. Even the psychiatrist's letter assuring him that II was fully aware of the consequences of my actions didn't instill confidence in her lawyer. He wasn't prepared to proceed with her offer to purchase the house in her name, fearing II might come to my senses and demand my portion of the sale. II ended up calling the lawyer to see what could be worked out. That's when II found out he had no idea II was dealing with a gender identity problem. After explaining my situation to him, he said he understood the motives behind my action but that he thought II was nuts, and then he offered to have one of his friends draw up the necessary wording for me to sign. Even this lawyer was hesitant. He tried counseling me to rethink

113

my action, since he didn't know any others who would voluntarily give up everything they had worked for all their lives. He too was afraid that II might turn around and sue him for bad advice when II came to my senses. Now an affidavit was required to protect the lawyer so II couldn't take action at a later date.

Once the lawyers were satisfied, then the bank got into the act. They wouldn't give my wife the mortgage she wanted because she had no credit rating. Of course she didn't. She had been a stay at home mom, but she held investments with the same bank in excess of the mortgage she was asking for. That didn't matter, they said, because she had no personal payment history. So in order for her to obtain the mortgage and leave her investments intact they required me to co-sign her mortgage.

In the middle of all this financial messing about, the long awaited letter from the Gender Clinic finally arrived. They had scheduled my evaluation to take place in two weeks. Their evaluation would require two days of thorough testing by a variety of specialists, psychiatrists, psychologists, sociologists, an endocrinologist and medical laboratory work ups. My state of limbo was going to end. Finally the end of a lifetime of dreams was in sight. II was going to get all my questions answered, the help II sought, and the advice II needed. The cure that would end this nightmare was only two weeks away.

Two weeks have never passed so slowly. II felt as though II was lying on the ground watching the grass grow. II wouldn't describe myself as a patient person. II had always felt that lineups were only for cattle being led to the slaughter. When II made up my mind to do something, II wanted to get at it and have it finished. On the Saturday before II was scheduled to arrive at the clinic II purchased the tickets for the two days so II could avoid any line ups at the bus station Monday morning. After buying the tickets and paying my rent for the month II was broke but happy that my nightmare was finally coming to an end.

II don't think II've ever been late for anything in my life. Monday morning my journal records that II was up at two-thirty to get ready to catch the bus at six. It was a good thing because the city buses didn't run at that time of the day, so II had to walk downtown to the bus terminal. II had only recently begun going out in public during the day time dressed as a female. At the bus terminal Monday morning II began feeling very self conscious and fearful about riding on a packed, male dominated commuter bus, all the way into Toronto, dressed as a female.

After arriving at the bus terminal in Toronto, II proceeded to walk to the clinic on College. II walked quickly with my head down so II wouldn't have to look into the people's faces as II passed by them. II arrived in front of the clinic with more than an hour to spare. Fortunately for me there was a little coffee shop next to the Clarke Institute where II could waste an hour or so drinking coffee. II didn't want to appear too eager, and besides II needed to build up my courage. After all, II had no idea what to expect.

Inside the main entrance II checked the directory by the elevator to find out where II needed to go. Ah, the fourth floor was the Gender Clinic. Stepping off the elevator, II was greeted by an arrow to the right and another to the left. To the right was the "Gender Clinic" and to the left "Sexual Deviance". What had II gotten myself into?

II found the reception desk around the corner and introduced myself to the receptionist. The young woman appeared to be a person just like II had dreamt of, a work in progress trans-sexual. Only her voice gave her away, which is one thing that trans-sexuals can seldom mask. Any attempt to raise one's voice artificially comes across sounding phony. For that reason II decided not to take this route and have tried to make the lower voice work in my favour. It has sort of become a conversation piece and my trademark. Of course there is also the option of surgery to alter the voice, but the expense doesn't justify the risk in my opinion. There are three possible outcomes: a perfectly female voice, no voice change, or worst of all, no voice at all.

It must have been the big city way of communicating, but she didn't appear very friendly when she sent me to sit in front of the elevator doors again. "Have a seat around the corner. We'll call you when we're ready for

116

you."

The seating area she referred to was directly opposite the elevator doors, common to both areas below the signs pointing left and right. As II sat there watching the elevator doors open and close, II tried to think what people standing on the elevator thought II was sitting there for. Was II a left or a right arrow? Was II a gender crisis or a sexual deviant? Eventually someone came to the end of the hall and called, "Mr. So and So."

Why did they have to subject me to further humiliation? It was bad enough sitting in front of the elevators and the overhead signs indicating II might be abnormal. Did they have to refer to me as Mr. when II was dressed in women's clothes?

II was taken into an office by a social worker. She explained the purpose and scope of the Gender Clinic, what would be required of me to complete the transition from male to female and the final surgery. Then she began typing my personal history and data into her computer file, all those little details that define you as a person, where you live, telephone number and so on. Was II still under the care of the psychiatrist that had made the referral? II asked her to change that part of the file to show the name of my current psychiatrist, since the name in their file was for the psychiatrist at Homewood. II requested that any communication should be directed to my current psychiatrist.

Then II began the rounds of all the specialists, two in

117

the morning and two in the afternoon. The same would happen the next day. The first was a sociologist. She probed my social behavior. How many sexual partners had II had? How many presently? Did II drink? Had II had same sex relations? Did II use street drugs? Had II been involved in criminal activity? She appeared shocked when II told her II had been married for thirty-two years to the same person and answered no to all of her other questions. II must have appeared a very dull person in her eyes.

The next was a psychiatrist. He was also the doctor in charge of the clinic. His first question? "Why are you here?"

"II want to live."

"Why didn't you come here long before this? How can we help you?"

"II need answers for me and help for my family to understand."

"If they don't understand now, they never will. You can lead them to water, but you can't make them drink. And as far as a cure, well, if it could be done I'd have won the Noble prize, and II haven't been nominated yet, so II guess it can't be done. People who claim they can reverse trans-sexuality and homosexuality really mean they can help the individuals suppress their inner identities and desires to take on society's approval. Eventually this repression breaks down and the condition resurfaces. There are only three tried and true ways of dealing with it. The

118

first is to kill yourself. The second is a miraculous intervention, but that isn't likely to happen. The third is to become a female. Those are your choices."

As he spoke these words, one part of me desperately wanted to be cured and return to the safe comfortable life of marriage and family. The other part of me knew that what he was saying was the only realistic option II had. But his sarcasm still stung. II don't know if it was his manner, his sarcasm, or that he was telling me what II didn't want to face, but II disliked him from that moment on, and it was only the beginning of the session. II tried to explain the spiritual conflict in my life surrounding this situation, but he had no understanding and couldn't accept that God could care one bit about my problem.

He called his secretary into the room, a woman older than me and not particularly well dressed. "What do you think of how he's dressed?" he asked her.

"Not very feminine," she said, and as if to shove the knife in a little deeper, "Sort of androgynous," she mumbled.

"That's what II thought too," he said.

This doctor really made me feel that there was little or no hope in the world left for me. All of a sudden he had turned into a fashion critic, and his sixty plus secretary could have benefited from a complete make over, beginning with her salt and pepper hair color. II on the other hand felt appropriately dressed as a middle aged woman in feminine slacks, nylons, low heels and a sweater. Be-

119

tween the two of them II wanted to get on the bus and go back home. II had come to this clinic looking for answers and help, but II had found neither.

The rest of the day didn't go much better. II was unable to find out what they expected of people in my situation. From the questions asked by the sociologist and by her comments about my life, II could assume that most tran-ssexuals must lead a very different life style from the one II had lived. They seemed surprised that II wasn't involved in substance abuse and multiple sexual partners with both genders. II felt II had failed her test, another put down, another rejection. II really didn't want to spend another day in that place.

The next day was a little different. There was more physical testing rather than the mind games of the day before. First on the schedule was the endocrinologist, the doctor responsible for my hormonal therapy. When II arrived at her waiting room, it was already full with people of all ages. The receptionist handed me a questionnaire to complete and return to her. One of the questions on the form asked what operations II had undergone. With no reason to expect otherwise, II listed everything including the angioplasty. Then II had to step up to her desk and answer some rather personal questions orally. II was uncomfortable standing there in front of all those people answering questions II had already answered the day before. Why couldn't the clinic pass all this the information along to the necessary specialists? Finally the doctor escorted me into an examination room and asked me to remove all of my clothes and climb up on the table. Then she left the room. After what seemed an eternity laying naked on the table, the door of the examination room opened. She moved over my body inspecting the genital area and my chest.

"Do you shave your body?" she asked.

"Just my underarms and legs," II answered.

"Not the pubic area? Are you sure?"

"No, just my underarms and legs," II replied again.

"Okay, get dressed."

That was it, no other questions. II'm amazed that in two minutes time she knew everything about me. Then II was off to a women's hospital for a battery of physical tests, blood work, x-rays, ultrasounds.

II returned to the Gender Clinic for an appointment with a psychologist who unfortunately had a schedule of appointments that was different from mine. He had been waiting twenty minutes for me to show and had become quite irritated that II was late. Our time was shortened, but he promised to read my file eventually. So much for his expertise and professionalism. How could this doctor have gained an insight into my psyche and my issues in one fifteen minute session.

Before leaving the Clinic II learned that the person II spoke to several months previously on the phone had not been truthful. They did have a support group that met every Wednesday evening at the Clinic and another support group was just beginning for family members.

That night when II arrived home II was convinced above all else that though II had gone to the clinic to get answers directly from the horse' mouth, II had ended up speaking to the wrong end of the horse instead. II was disillusioned with the Clinic. They had been no help to me whatsoever. They gave me nothing to hope for. It was mainly a cold impersonal group of egotistical and arrogant quasi-professionals masquerading as experts. In my business life II had been given the opportunity to speak at several conferences, and II never wanted to be introduced as an expert in my particular field. II had always regarded experts as people carrying briefcases a hundred miles away from where anyone knew them.

The future of my life now lay in the hands of people II didn't know or particularly trust. Later that month they would hold a conference of all the doctors who had seen me during the two days of testing to evaluate my life. They said that II could also attend this conference and learn first hand what recommendations were to be forthcoming. After a couple of weeks II had heard nothing from the Clinic, so II enquired. They hadn't got around to scheduling the conference yet, II was told. After a few more weeks, there was still no word, so II contacted them again. This time they had already had the conference and in the intervening two weeks they had changed their policy to exclude the client from the conference.

They had mailed out their report.

II finally tracked down the Clinic's report. They had mailed it to the Homewood doctor rather than the doctor II had requested during my visit to the Clinic. Since the hospital doctor's file was closed, the report ended up in the hospital's record department. II had to pay the record department at Homewood for a copy of the report. When II finally got my hands on it, there, in big bold letters across the top, it read, "NOT TO BE SHOWN TO PATIENT".

II think my first response was anger. My second was despondence. How could they do this to me? As II read and reread that report, II noticed that it had been authored by seven people who sat in judgement of my life. II had only been interviewed by one of the people named in the report, and guess who that was? It was the sarcastic doctor who headed up the Clinic and hadn't yet been nominated for the Nobel prize. He alone decided who would be treated and who would not. It was apparent that II wasn't going to receive much help from the Clinic.

Although the report confirmed the diagnosis that II was a trans-sexual, it didn't recommend feminization at that time. It was cut and dried. They offered no other hope whatsoever.

After II regained my composure, II felt the Clinic had essentially signed my death warrant. How could II hope to make the change without their assistance? That day everything in my life lay in ruin and rubble. Essentially everything was gone. My dream had been shattered by a few words on a piece of paper. They hadn't even bothered to provide an explanation. After II had a good cry, II took the report to my psychiatrist. II wanted him to know why II was feeling so rejected and empty.

My doctor and II discussed the report, and he saw no medical reason why II couldn't proceed on my own without the help of the Clinic. He also encouraged me to challenge the Clinic report. II sent the Clinic a letter asking for an explanation of their recommendation, but they chose to remain silent and have never responded. The clinic endocrinologist did respond but outright lied, giving me a false hope that II would be able to begin my hormonal treatment. She promised time and again to provide the necessary prescription. Eventually II gave up on her promises.

As a result of this shabby treatment and what II considered to be unorganized and unprofessional treatment by the Clinic, II decided to take my concerns to the Health Services Appeal Board a year after II had completed my reassignment surgery. Unfortunately II did not win my argument for financial compensation to cover the cost of my reassignment surgery, and four months after the Board's decision, the Ontario Government withdrew all funding for sexual reassignment surgery in the province. II agree wholeheartedly with their decision. One of the requirements for sexual reassignment surgery is an overwhelming desire to have the surgery, and II believe that means wanting it at any cost. Instead of taking out a loan for a car, it may be necessary to invest in yourself by taking a loan for your surgery. People invest in their future by taking out student loans, why not sexual reassignment surgery loans?

With the fiasco of the Gender Clinic behind me, II left in a state of despondence. II wasn't exactly sure which way to turn. The one way II was pretty sure I didn't want to turn was backward. Emotionally II felt tossed to and fro. Was it satanic influences? Was it because II missed the security and stability of the family? Or was it simply the uncertainty of being released from my prison? The next few months were pivotal as II wrestled again with God, myself and the family.

The sale of our home had signaled the final demise of a marriage relationship that had come apart at the seams already. The week before Easter that year II went home to make a few last repairs around the house before the new owners took possession. As II looked around the house, it was like slipping on a comfortable pair of shoes. My mind flooded with memories as II looked at the bumps and scratches from twenty-two years of family life. In the garage II could still picture the car engines hanging from the I-beam while the boys waited for parts from some scrap yard. The grease stains on the floor were silent sentinels of long forgotten old cars that were once the pride and joy of teenage boys. There was also a deep sense of loss as II realized this would probably be the last time II would stand in the midst of so many memories.

II had resolved to use the weekend to dispose of all those photos, mementoes and tokens that recorded my past. II wanted nothing left behind that could be used as a reminder and testimony of the pain of the past fifty years. That day it had all become meaningless junk.

After the work was done, my wife and II finally sat down to discuss the Clarke Gender tests and the only solutions they could offer to end the nightmare in my life. It was evident from her tears that her nightmare had just been intensified. The tears said it all, but the words confirmed the pain tearing her apart.

II wished II could have offered her comfort and reassurance that our lives would turn out some other way. II wanted to hold her and tell her everything would be okay, but it would only have been a lie. As II sat in the quietness of the dark after she had gone to bed, II felt some relief knowing that II had finally been open and honest about the direction our lives were taking.

The next day II had planned to speak to all the kids and tell them the same things that my wife and II had discussed the previous night, but they weren't all available at the same time. II didn't want to do it piecemeal. It would be better if everyone knew at the same time.

The following Sunday was Easter, and my wife invited me to join the family for Easter dinner. It would be a special occasion as the last family dinner to be held in our old home. The day already had a dark cloud hanging over it, and my appearance didn't add any rays of sunshine. As II entered the house II immediately sensed the tension and uneasiness my presence created. II suspected that my sons were already aware of the reason II was there. They glowered at the length of my hair. My sisters-in-law barely acknowledged my presence. II truly felt like a skunk in the cabbage patch. II should have turned and walked away, but II had to speak to the kids about my intention to make the separation from my wife permanent. II had asked the kids to remain after the meal so we could talk when every one else had left, but some of them had to leave early, so we had to go for a walk to find privacy from the rest of the family. As II began to explain the Clinic's suggestions, they admitted they already knew all there was to know. Our time together was both tense and emotional. We expressed love for one another, but they couldn't agree with my decision. The only acceptable option was that II return to the family as the father they had known and the grandfather they wanted for their children.

That was the last time my sons and II spoke, except for my one son who came to visit me a couple of months later in a final effort to try and persuade me that my choices were wrong. When he left he gave me this letter, which II treasure because of his honesty, his openness to confront his dad, to speak the truth in love and in the power of Christ working in his life.

June 22/95

Dear Dad,

I am writing this journal to let you know the impact
that your decision has had on my wife and I. You once
told me the importance of keeping a journal in business
so that I had a record of all the things said during conversations. This journal is not so much for record, but
to some how let you know the pain I deal with on a daily
basis. I should have started this a few weeks ago when
mom moved because that day was very hard. Hard for a
few reasons. One I felt without you there that we were
packing up and leaving you behind, when in fact you
had already left us behind, and as I sat on my bedroom
floor with tears flowing down my face I realized just how
much your decisions have cost. Today was another hard
day and it may seem silly but it is just another thing
that I realized. I had taken my wife out for lunch and as
I sat there I noticed an older man eating lunch and it reminded me of you. He looked so alone and as I watched,
I remembered those days when you would come to the
school to pick me up and take me out to lunch. Boy, I
sure felt like a big shot when I told my friends that my
dad was taking me out to lunch. And as I remembered,
it hit me with tears in my eyes that there is not going
to be a day when I can call up my father and say, hey
dad, how about I take you to lunch. You know dad that
I love you, but these decisions have hurt me deeply and
robbed me of a father. You see dad, God has already
given me a mother whom I love and hold great respect
for. I don't need another. What I need even at 27 is a
father, the father God gave me.

You see dad, no matter how much you try to change your manner and your appearance, one thing will remain. God made you my father and me your son and nothing will ever change this! Dad please remember that I will always love you no matter the cost, not because it is easy, but it is what God has commanded of me.

Love always, Your son.

8

II Don't Need Enemies.
II Have Friends.

During the next several months some of my longtime friends learned about my nasty big secret. One by one they tried last ditch stands for righteousness' sake. If only they could persuade me that my decision was wrong, both for myself and the family. They would have liked to accomplish God's will for my life, as they saw it, by having me give up on my desire to become a female. II find it amazing how we always have the right insight into someone else's dilemma but seldom into our own. Just like my family, they didn't even want to learn anything about who II was, why and how long I had put up with this conundrum in my life.

One friend invited me for a drive up to his cottage for the day. The six hours we sat in the car gave us ample opportunity to discuss my situation and the direction II had chosen for my life. He wasn't too sure II was making the right choice. He felt he understood my pain, but he also felt that by forging ahead II would only provide myself with temporary relief. He believed that gender identity was reversible with good Christian counseling. He asked if II would be open to this avenue if he could find such a counselor. So far nothing had been carved in stone, and yes, II would take any opportunity to have this situation end, but II had one condition. The counselor must not be biased toward sexual problems, because what II was experiencing was not a sexual problem. When he dropped me off at my apartment that evening, it was the last time we ever spoke.

For the next few months II was visited by a number of old friends and church members. They basically couldn't comprehend why II was doing this terrible thing and hurting my family this way. They couldn't see why, if II had been able to live all those years with my secret, II couldn't just continue without these changes. They never understood, and II dare say they didn't want to understand my pain or the hurts that had wounded me. It seems the only hurt that had any significance was their own.

My one sister felt much the same way. Why, for mom's sake, couldn't II just put my life on hold until mom went home to be with the Lord. Then mom wouldn't have to experience the hurt of my decision.

My one friend came to visit and asked, "Are you gay?"

"Well that depends, doesn't it?" II replied.

How could II truthfully answer his question with a

simple yes or no. II saw myself as a female. Therefore, if II was attracted to a male, in my mind II wasn't gay. On the other hand, because II had a male body and was attracted to a male, then yes, in a sense II must be gay.

"No, II'm not gay," II answered, "because II can't allow myself to be attracted to either gender, and for that reason the doctors say II'm asexual. Why do you ask?"

"Because if you were gay, then I couldn't visit you. People might get the wrong impression of me."

"Well, what do you think their impression will be when they learn you're visiting a man who thinks he's a woman?" II shot back.

His visit was extremely short that day. He left shortly after our little discussion, and he took the microwave he had loaned me. He never came to visit again. His remarks startled and hurt me. How could a Christian person sit there and say such garbage? But, all too often they do. II've done it. Too often Christians interpret the biblical instruction to discern as an instuction to judge. Perhaps we would do better to engage our minds before we condemn ourselves with our mouths.

Because II was a man in appearance when II moved into the seniors' apartment building, some residents became confused when II started my transition. They had seen a man move in, and suddenly there was a funny looking woman coming and going from the apartment. Several of the residents became incensed about my pres-

133

ence and often referred to me as the "He/She" in an audible voice, loud enough for me to hear them. They approached the building managers about this "He/She" living in their building, requesting that II be evicted. Fortunately II had sent a letter to the management company advising them of my new legal identity and the purpose for the change. The managers defended my right to live in whatever way II saw fit and advised the residents of my situation, suggesting that if they couldn't handle my presence then perhaps they would have to make a decision about their residency in the building. As it turned out II don't believe anyone changed their residency on my account, and over time many of the people there have become my friends.

One of my neighbors chided me by asking, "I don't know why you'd want to become a woman. There's a shortage of good men already." How true! Now that II would like to begin a relationship with a man, a good one is hard to find.

There are a few people who, no matter what, still regard me as an oddball. This seems to give them the permission to mistreat me simply because II have failed to meet their standards. Usually it only involves stares or strange faces in my direction. Sometimes there's verbal abuse involving derogatory names, but then there are those who are so weak in their own identity that they resort to physical abuse in order to prove their own worthiness. While II was growing up we kids used to say,

"Sticks and stones will break my bones, but names will never hurt me." The truth is that they both hurt. One leaves a physical scar, the other an invisible one.

One wet fall evening, as II was returning home after spending a day at the psychiatric self help group, II heard the sound of running footsteps and yelling coming from behind me. They were yelling, "Faggot" and "Queer" and making obscene gestures. As II turned, an elbow landed on the side of my head, knocking my glasses off and forcing me to the ground. II instinctively went into the fetal position as II hit the sidewalk. They were immediately kicking and punching and shouting all the more their obscenities. II lay there, hurt, bleeding and aching. Surely someone would see what was happening and help me, but no one came. That night II wished II had taken the bus, but in those days II generally walked everywhere to save money. Finally they had their fill and ran off laughing. They had defeated a queer faggot. Thankfully it only occurred once, but once is enough to gain an appreciation of the abuse that minorities such as gays and lesbians fear every time they walk down the street.

II had bought myself a second hand lady's watch at the recycle shop, but it needed a new battery. While in the mall one day, II took it into a major department store. As the salesman approached the counter, he said, "Yes Ma'am, how can I help you?"

"Well, II'd like my watch battery replaced please."

"Yes, Sir," he said. "It'll only take a few minutes. Do you want to wait?"

"No, II'll be back in half an hour," II told him.

When II returned to his counter, he said again, "Yes Ma'am, how can I help you?"

"II'm here to pick up my watch."

"Oh, yes Sir, oh, I'm sorry." He was obviously embarrassed.

"That's okay," II said, "II have a habit of confusing people. Actually II'm the bass singer for the girls' quartet."

However, there are also times when II have lost my patience when people have difficulty with my appearance not being consistent with my voice. II went to the drugstore in the neighborhood to pick up my monthly prescriptions. At the cash register II encountered a young girl who broke out in the giggles and just couldn't refocus herself when II tried to greet her.

"Do you think II'm funny?" I asked her. There was no reply. "My family doesn't." The smirk disappeared from her face. The druggist who was standing nearby said nothing, but II never saw the young girl again.

After finishing at the psychiatric survivors one day, II decided to treat myself to the best hamburger in town. The little diner on the main street makes a hamburg so big that half of the meat hangs outside the bun on each end. The waitress took my order and made a comment about my deep sexy female voice that wasn't very discreet. Before she typed the order into the computer, II watched as she pointed me out to all of the other staff. Shortly there was a parade of the other staff past my table. II had just become the evening's entertainment, but II had the last laugh. II made sure she had to make change so that II could leave a tip. Instead, II put all the change in my purse, took out my pen and wrote on the back of the receipt:

"Thank you for such fine service. But since you made me tonight's entertainment, I charge for my services, so I have kept your tip as payment. Have a great evening."

One day while II was volunteering at the psychiatric center, my friend Father John called in a panic. He needed me to take over the office at the conference center right away. He had an urgent family crisis, and a group was due to arrive at any time. He needed me to come immediately. II explained that II was completely dressed as a female, and if that was okay with him II could come. He said he didn't have a problem with it, and he'd come right away to pick me up. Within ten minutes he had dropped me off at the conference center, and he was gone.

II started making the preparations for the group coming in by checking that all the rooms were ready. II took a short cut to the bedroom area through the rented office space of a nursing organization. As II passed through their office, II heard someone shriek, but II didn't pay much attention and just continued on my way. Shortly after II returned to the conference center office, II had a visitor. The priest in charge of the complex came in and closed the door behind him. The closed door, the look on his face, and the shriek II had heard all indicated this wasn't a social call.

"We can't have you here in our building dressed in this fashion. We must be sensitive to what people think. I don't want you here dressed as anything but a man."

"But II can't do that," II said. "II won't even do that for my own family any more. II will not compromise myself for anyone."

"Then please leave, and don't come back."

That year my daughter and daughter-in-law had accepted my invitation to bring the grandchildren for a picnic to celebrate my birthday. The day before the picnic II received a surprise phone call from an old pastor friend who now lived on the west coast. He had been the counseling pastor at the church before he went into private practice. He said he had received a phone call from my wife, who was quite upset at the prospect of the grandchildren coming to visit. He was in complete agreement with her. He believed that if II made contact with my grandchildren, II would surely destroy them mentally for the rest of their lives. At first II wondered about his opinion, but II respected this man, so II agreed to cancel the planned picnic. However, looking back, II did the wrong thing, though for what II thought was the right reason. II lied to my daughter as to why II canceled the picnic. II didn't want her to know that II had called off the picnic with the kids basically at the request of her mother through the pastor.

It seemed that everyone knew best how II should live my life, but II truly believe not one of them knew the impact this gender thing was having on my life. II can't believe any of them ever stopped to learn or consider just what the term 'gender identity' means. By speaking out they merely confirmed their ignorance. When II refused to submit to their thinking, my friends' visits stopped, and our friendships ceased, as did my relationship with my sister. Even though the whole family knew that II felt like a female when II was released from Homewood, they were prepared to help me until II declared that II was going to begin living full time as a female.

The pastor's call was the final straw. All this time II had been sitting on the papers that would be the largest step to a new identity. II had been procrastinating again. II decided then and there as II hung up the phone that it was now time to move ahead.

Several months previously II had contacted the Registrar General's Office for the province and received the necessary documents to change my name to an unambiguously female one. II had hesitated to return the paperwork for two reasons, one financial, because the cost was going to consume my living allowance for another month, and the other psychological, because from that point forward II would be shutting and locking the gate behind me.

Before the paperwork could be completed, there had to be a verification of police records and an affirmation that there were no outstanding charges or judgements against me in the courts. When the paperwork was completed, II stood at the mail box, licked the stamp and dropped the envelope into the slot. II watched as it slid down into the box. II knew there was no turning back from this point. Within weeks II received my new birth certificate and a completely new legal identity. II was now legally, "Janet Elizabeth Manne, Male".

When II told my doctor about changing my family name, he immediately saw through my twisted sense of humor. One of the reasons for choosing Manne for my new family name, , besides the play on words, was because in old English it meant a servant. That is how II would like my life to be remembered, not as someone who was different, but as someone who wanted to serve others with whatever gifts and talents God had entrusted to me. My life up until then had been focused on 'things'. Things don't talk back. They don't pry into your life, and they don't get up close up and personal. For my new life II wanted to change that cold impersonal part of my life and become a heart person.

With the revised birth certificate II could now change all the other legal documentation, driver's licence, social insurance number, pension funds, apartment lease. However, II made a bad decision by not changing my health

140

card to the new photo I.D. at that time. To do so meant the cost of a bus trip to another city, because it was the only location in the area where this could obtained. Every time II went to the medical testing laboratory, which was frequently, II had to show my health card then wait in their crowded waiting room until they called my name. Of all the medical offices II had to visit they were the only one who refused to acknowledge me as Janet, this despite the fact that the request from the doctor was made out for Janet. Each time II went there II knew that II would be embarrassed. Invariably they called out my male name, and II had to respond to it dressed as a female.

Within a short five month period after II announced my intention to fully become a female, II had completely alienated all of my family and my friends. My support now rested with Father John, the psychiatrist, and a couple of biological females that II had met through the psychiatric survivor consumer group.

II was beginning to realize that II was being unrealistic in thinking that people had more to do with their lives than to be concerned with how II was living mine. My presence was shocking to the people II encountered for a while. II was expecting them either to ignore me or to be tolerant of me, but it didn't work that way. One way or another II had to provide an option for people to feel more at ease and not feel threatened by something foreign to their experience. II began using a little bit of humor when II encountered them. That way II could break the ice without putting myself down and still be able to express what they were afraid to say.

9
Slow and Easy

Now Ahab the Arab had been traveling several days with his trusty camel, and the sun was reaching that point where Ahab would have to call it a day. He tapped the camel's front leg with his rod to have the camel kneel so he could dismount. Then he fastened the leg bridle to the camel and drove the holding stake into the hot sand.

Ahab rolled out his prayer carpet facing to the east and said his evening prayers. When he had finished, he tended to his camel with food and drink. Then he pitched his shelter and made his evening meal. The sun had already set, and the darkness had fallen on Ahab and the desert like a blanket. As he prepared for the night he checked that his camel was secured with the leg tether, and he gazed at the sky and marveled at the beauty of Alla's heavens.

Shortly after retiring, Ahab felt a nuzzle against his shoulder. It was his camel, asking if he could put his nose in the tent, for the warm desert air of the day was turning cold tonight. So Ahab had compassion, and the camel was allowed to keep his nose in the tent. Later the camel nuzzled Ahab again, and the camel asked if it would be okay to put his head in the tent because his eyes were beginning to water from the chill of the night air. Again Ahab agreed.

When Ahab awoke in the morning, he was shivering and chilled through and through. As he opened his eyes, he realized he had been pushed out the rear of the tent. During the night his companion, the camel, hadn't bothered Ahab anymore to ask permission. He had assumed that if he inched his way into the tent, Ahab wouldn't notice his encroachment .

You're probably asking, "What the heck does all this have to do with me changing my gender?"

It was a story my psychiatrist shared with me after II made my final decision to make the change. He thought the best way for me to go about making the changes in my life, dress and thinking was slowly. If II acted like the camel and inched my way through the changes, II would probably upset the least number of people at any one time.

Granny used to tell me, God helps those who help themselves. Now you won't find these words in the Bible, at least II haven't found them yet, but there is some truth in this saying. Some people believe that if they sit and wait long enough, or pray hard enough, eventually God will make things happen in their lives, but God can't steer the car if the engine isn't running and in gear.

In some ways II believe the decision for my life was

made a long time ago, in Nova Scotia, when II planned to disappear to England. At the time II just didn't know how to go about it, and II was too fearful to talk to anyone. Instead II sat on it for all those wasted years, hoping in the back of my mind that my problems would all miraculously go away. But now my decision was firmly made. Forget the Clinic. II could ill afford to wait around for their arbitrary whims. After all, the only benefit they offered was their exclusive monopolistic arrangement with the Ontario Hospital Insurance Plan. Only those persons recommended by the Clinic for surgical sexual reassignment could have the cost of the operation approved for payment by OHIP.

For me to proceed on my own meant the cost of the surgery would be totally my responsibility. It also reduced the waiting to only one year as opposed to the three to five years at the Gender Clinic. With the help of my psychiatrist II set about arranging for the necessary specialists and putting together a properly monitored program. He was able to locate a key person in the program, another trans-sexual in the area, and to arrange for us to meet one another. She had been in the Clinic's program for five years at that time and was on the verge of leaving their program to finish the transition and surgery on her own. Her knowledge and her experience were most helpful to us in setting up my program.

A couple of months before my final decision II wanted to begin the hormonal therapy, but II was unsure how my family doctor was going to react if II asked for a prescription for estrogen. At that time II had not divulged my gender identity conflict to her. Rather than risk the humiliation of being rejected, II went to the library and searched through text books and manuals on herbal remedies because II had seen a magazine advertisement for a herb reported to be a natural estrogen. The herb, Blue Cohosh Root, was also called papoose root and squaw root. II purchased a small amount of this herb in the local health food store and began making a tea as recommended in the library book. How effective it was over the short period of time II took it, II'm not sure. Psychologically it benefited me to feel that at least II was doing something. With my final decision made, II took the giant leap and visited my family doctor, pouring out my heart to her, armed with the Clinic report and the information II had been able to glean concerning estrogen therapy for trans-sexual males.

Through her II received prescriptions for estrogen and an androgen blocker plus a referral to an endocrinologist to monitor the hormonal therapy. Trans-sexual hormonal therapy consists of large doses of estrogen in the range of four to six times what a biological female would be administered for hormone replacement therapy. The androgen blocker, as the name suggests, blocks the male hormone androgen, to retard hair growth. It also has the effect of reducing the testicles. II eventually had to stop the androgen blocker because the doctors were afraid that there would be insufficient tissue to perform sexual reassignment surgery if II continued on this medication. The estrogen therapy is required for various functions, including fat distribution, breast enlargement, changes to the texture of the skin. However, estrogen has no effect on the male voice. Neither does tight underwear, II might add. Estrogen therapy is usually the initial step transsexuals take in transforming their lives. It is one step that can be taken that is reversible, and it can be taken with no one else's knowledge.

It seemed the time had come for my post graduate trans-sexual education to begin. This meant day after day spending time at the local malls, watching and studying the social graces of the female gender. Some of the little idiosyncracies II was already familiar with, for instance, holding up a line of irritated male shoppers while looking for the exact change at a check-out even if it meant emptying my purse to do it. There were important lessons like stopping to greet a friend at the bottom of an escalator or in the middle of a doorway, or like walking through a doorway without looking back to see if someone else was coming after me. There were important lessons in how to sit, keeping my legs crossed, rising gracefully from one of those chairs that had enfolded me. II also learned to eat by taking nibbles and wiping the corners of my mouth to prevent lipstick from caking at the corners of my lips.

During that transition period many people were curious about which washroom II would use. "Whichever one doesn't have a lineup," II'd answer. Actually II had to be careful. II rarely used the washrooms unless II was accompanied by one of my biologically female friends. II didn't want someone mistaking my voice and thinking that there was a pervert in the women's washroom. Besides, it's illegal for one gender to use the other gender's washroom facilities. But you can be sure of one thing, there was no way II would enter a men's room dressed as a female.

Then followed the more visible changes. II had allowed my hair to grow longer, and II needed to have it cut and styled. II think my fear on that first trip into the beauty parlor was the same fear a young boy experiences the first time he sits in the barber shop chair. The only difference is that he can cry and scream, but II had to hide my embarrassment. II hung around the mall until an hour before the shop closed, trying to be sure II'd be the only one in the shop. The stylist had me made right away.

"How long have you been in your transition?" she asked.

"II'm just starting."

"I've met several who have gone through the process."

She eased my nervousness as we continued to discuss what she knew from her past experiences.

Next II wanted to remove what little facial hair II had. After my experience in Newfoundland, II wasn't about to repeat the same mistake with a facial hair remover. That's when II investigated electrolysis. II had no idea what II was getting myself into. II'm deathly afraid of bees, and II tend to freak when II encounter them. Well, II learned that electrolysis is like having a bee sting you about six times a minute for thirty minutes to an hour per session. Even with the little bit of facial hair that II had, they estimated it would take about two years of treatment. Then II found out that not every hair is permanently killed. It depends on the stage of growth for each individual hair.

This sparked my curiosity about the questions the Clinic endocrinologist had asked about whether II shaved in the pubic area. II obtained library books dealing with the subject of hair growth and hair patterns. Sure enough, my bodily hair growth patterns were not typical for a male body. The male pattern of body hair cones upward from the pelvic area to the chest, the female hair pattern goes straight across at the pelvic area. No wonder she was curious. My bodily hair was almost negligible in all the areas where most males would have hair growth. None of the books offered a less painful alternative for permanent hair removal than electrolysis.

Next step. A new pair of glasses with more feminine frames were in order. As II stood in front of the mirror trying on frames and looking at myself in the mirror, twisting my head this way and that, II felt the eyes of the whole store turn in my direction. Then the moment of

149

truth, my final selection and the long walk to the counter. When II started to speak, II knew that II was the focus of attention. II glanced sideways out of the corner of my eye to see heads shaking and lips pursed in disgust. Would there ever come a time when II would loose this fear and self consciousness?

10
II've Got Questions

In the twelve month period following my release from the psychiatric center II battled with the guilt of hurting my family. II was obsessed with the fear of what people thought of me. II knew my choices were few and far between. II wanted to live, but not in the way II had lived my life so far. Frankly II was tired of just fighting to stay alive.

These pressures were nothing compared to the battle raging inside my mind and spirit. My fundamental Christian beliefs were at war with my intellect. II couldn't understand why a loving, merciful God could hate me this much, to permit this duplicitous spirit in my life. There were times II would have rather denied God's existence then to deal with myself on the questions of moral right and wrong, black and white thinking.

God, is there really such a thing as sin?

If there is, is it your yardstick of my worth?

The more II tried to answer these questions the less sure II was about anything, except that II always came back to the literalist thinking of right/wrong, black/white, and these flew in the face of my desire to be a female. The only thing II knew for sure was that II didn't ever want to go back into the past of lies, deceit and closet living. For the last twenty years or so II had been taught that II would know my decisions were in the center of God's will when II felt peace about them. At the time II made my decision to change my physical gender, II didn't particularly feel a sense of peace, nor did II sense a feeling of peace when II decided to live in the closet. Obviously there must be more to knowing God's plan for my life than just sensing peace. After all, II had also been taught and scolded for living by my unstable feelings.

God, perhaps you've noticed that II have a lot of unanswered questions.

What is man?

Why can't II get you to answer?

Why won't you intervene when II'm making wrong decisions?

Will II ever find happiness?

Why do II feel guilty?

Are my desires selfish, as others want me think?

When will my torment end?

II desperately wanted to restore a relationship with God, but at the same time II didn't feel worthy. My volunteer work with the psychiatric survivors gave me a renewed sense of self worth and the feeling that in some small way II was using whatever abilities II had to serve God. My apartment had become known as Aunt Janet's, a refuge where many of these people could crash safely when they refused to take their meds, or needed a meal, or simply needed encouragement and confirmation that someone loved them. Was my help effective? II don't know. All II could do was offer friendship.

Father John and my psychiatrist were my islands of refuge from the mental storms raging inside me. It was evident to them that II needed spiritual healing within my soul and a fresh look at the things II believed. Mentally II questioned why Father John and II saw things so differently when we talked about the same God. At times it seemed we were talking about a God with a split personality, one holy, loving, kind and forgiving, the other holy, judgmental, demanding and punishing. By exploring the characteristics of our common God it became evident that He is all this and so much more. What was the difference then? Why did II see a dual personality God? Simply put, it was my personal focus. II had no trouble finding what II expected to find.

Part of my problem was that II had been taught the Bible as the literal word of God, and consequently II was steeped in the legalism of following all the biblical commandments literally. This created a feeling of worthlessness in my life, because II couldn't comply with all the rules and regulations. Father John was going to have a difficult time budging me from my 'literal perch'.

He felt II needed to deal with this 'literal perch' of mine before we could ever make any inroads into revising

153

my thinking process. Together we compared the various translations that had been written through the generations and compared them to one another and against the ancient Greek and Hebrew writings. What II learned shocked me. The meaning of simple English words had changed through the centuries, making it necessary in some cases to coin new English words that had never existed. Some of the translations actually added confusion and misinterpretation when they tried to make the original more understandable. New ways of expressing a passage were introduced to meet cultural differences. All in all II finally had to agree with the evidence. How could the Bible be the literal dictated word of God? It seemed more likely that it was inspired by God, capturing eternal truths. It was a huge step for me even to consider this possibility. II felt like II was balancing on one leg, teetering back and forth on a pile of stones. Any second everything could end up in a pile of rubble at my feet, and then II wouldn't have any foundation for my belief system.

Slowly, week after week, II let go of the literal concept of the Bible, but it opened other questions. It had been easy to judge something as black and white before, because the Bible said it was so. Now II alone was responsible to determine for my own life what was black or white, or if there was maybe a shade of grey.

For nearly twenty-five years II had been in turmoil over one biblical passage.

> A woman shall not wear anything that pertains to a
> man, nor shall a man put on a woman's garment; for
> whoever does these things is an abomination to the Lord
> your God. - Deuteronomy 22:5

This law was sandwiched in the middle of some mosaic social and cultural laws. It appears only the once in the Bible. Why was it stuck in there anyway? As II say, it haunted me, and it vilified me, and it irritated me. Obviously it's okay in our society today for women to wear men's clothes but not vice versa. Most commentaries explained that it was a cultural law in the time of the Old Testament, but every time II tried to get Father John to explain it away, he'd simply ask,

"Why do you need to know?"

II guess II really didn't need to know why it was there. Perhaps II wouldn't feel so guilt ridden if II could simply say that it didn't apply to my life today.

Father John saw the question as a greater teaching tool. One night we were talking about subjects along this line when he asked with a smile, not a smirk on his face:

"Do you belong to the New Testament or the Old Testament church? How did you enjoy your toasted bacon and tomato sandwich for lunch?"

"II enjoyed it. It's one of my favorites, but II like mayonnaise on it."

"I guess you must belong to the 'Pick and Choose'

church then," he chided.

As we talked, II began to understand his point. There are absolute spiritual commands given by God, and there are many cultural and societal requirements, and then there are a great many suggestions given in the Bible that will benefit our lives. The bacon on my sandwich was not an issue for me, but for others it might be. Would II be condemned by God for eating the bacon in spite of the biblical commandment not to eat meat from an animal with a cloven hoof? Not likely. So why was it still in the Bible as a don't do thing? II don't profess to have all the answers, but for me bacon is a non-issue.

There was another major hurdle II had to get over. We began discussing what constituted a man in my opinion. How did II define a man? What parameters defined man as God created? These questions were deeper than II had ever stopped to consider. A man is a man, and a woman is a woman. Right? Wrong! Or at least, that depends on what makes a man and a woman a woman.

II didn't want to think about these questions, and so II simply ignored them in preference of my literal perch. If II was born with male sexual organs at birth, how could II be anything else? Obviously there had to be some mysteries at work, somewhere, or else how did II get to where II was?

Father John said II was living in a narrow range of thought, again black/white, two states, male/female. There had been no room for me to consider any other condition as being valid for each gender. He pointed out that some men are so filled with maleness that they become male chauvinists, while some women are so feminine that they are looked upon as air heads. Not very flattering labels mind you, but then again some females go to the other extreme of being tom boyish and some males become sissies. And then there is the whole range of human gender in between these extremes. However, a greater percentage of each gender fall midway between these extreme characteristics along a continuum for each gender, as he called it.

The question II needed to be sure of was, "Does God care where on the continuum your life sits?" No! You are his creation, molded by the unique environment that He knew existed in your life and that has molded your life. Unless of course you prefer to believe, as some Christians do, that the Bible is the literal word of God, and then they might condemn everything sexual about your life.

II was beginning to understand so much more about this God II had paid lip service to over the years. My psychiatrist confirmed what Father John had been explaining. He took human gender and sexuality into the medical and scientific realm by explaining how our various gender components fit together to create a unique individual. Basically we have a gender identity (how we see our selves male/female), a gender role (what functions we are comfortable performing), a gender partner (the gender we are attracted to), a gender chemistry (male/female or both in special cases).

The combinational effects of these various gender components in a person fall along a gender continuum, ranging from one extreme to the other. II was slowly beginning to understand the psychological, psychiatric and chemical reasons that II thought of myself the way II did. II wasn't a reprobate. II wasn't demon possessed. II wasn't a sinful reject as some people had labeled me.

In the fall of that year, the church II had previously attended sent me a letter confirming the withdrawal of my membership from their body. II was yearning for a spiritual family. A friend invited me to attend a church service at the Rainbow Community Church one Sunday evening. She said the church was gay positive and was reaching out to disenfranchised Christians just like me, a church service where it was safe for gays, lesbians and trans-sexual people to worship. At first II was hesitant and nervous. II have to admit that I was homophobic. What might II encounter? How could they be Christian believers?

My spirit was crying out for Christian fellowship and corporate worship. II had tried mainline churches and always seemed to run into the same stone wall of rejection. II felt as welcome as a crow in the corn field, or maybe it was because they saw me as the scarecrow. How was II going to sit there in a church service and focus on God while they sat there focused on me, wondering just what kind of queer I was? On my way out after the service at

158

one church, II went up to introduce myself to the pastor as he greeted people at the door. As II approached him, II felt his eyes piercing right through me, as though he was trying to undress me. When my friend and I reached the outside, she asked,

"Did you see the way he looked you up and down?"

"Yes, II felt humiliated. II felt that he was trying to undress me with his eyes to see what II am."

II had virtually given up on mainline and evangelical churches. II spoke to several ministers about how they thought II would be accepted and fit into their congregations. They were anything but encouraging.

My friend had offered me the opportunity for corporate worship, but II wasn't sure that these people could be Christians. Look who was doing the discrimination now. II've had trouble more than once giving in to God's direction for my path. In my mind II could imagine all sorts of things that were going to take place at the church that night.

We entered the church, and II thought my friend had been joking that it was a gay positive church. There was no evidence to support the fears that II had conjured up in my mind. The service was a unique mixture of Evangelical, Anglican and Baptist. Oh, how comfortable II felt. The pastor gave a clear gospel message. They welcomed me as II had not been welcomed in any other church in the city. No one noticed or cared that II was a trans-sexual. God had found me a resting place. II felt

159

II was home at last.

II had tried to spend time each morning conversing with God and practicing what II had learned in the apple grove, listening. The day that II made my final decision to proceed with the reconstruction project, II read the prayer from my daily devotional book. It read,

> Thank you, Lord, for inner strength to pursue goals I established through wise counsel and prayer, rather than simply trying to please others... Amen.

Each day the prayer was also accompanied by a practice portion. On that day it read,

> "Today I refuse to allow the memory of a painful experience or failure to bind me in a dark shroud of dejection and defeat."

As II listened with my heart, II heard a small voice say, "It's okay to be yourself. Haven't I been there with you through all of this pain? The worst of all fears is the fear you create needlessly for yourself, and I haven't given you a spirit of fear. I have broken your chains today. Don't weld them back up again."

11
II Didn't Know That

My decision was made. II was ready to take that last
giant step in becoming a female. The surgeon's clinic in
Montreal was only a phone call away. Within a week they
had sent all the necessary requirements, forms and instructions. Only one obstacle stood in my way. II didn't
have all the necessary funds. II was short a few thousand dollars. What did II have to loose by not asking
the bank for a loan? After all, this was simply an investment II needed to make, and II had always thought
that the purpose of banks was to make investments. II
made an appointment with the loan officer at my bank
and told her II needed to borrow a few thousand dollars
for an investment II was making. When II arrived at the
bank, she greeted me with a big smile and ushered me
into her office. On her desk sat the center of the banking
business, her computer screen, showing all the financial
benefits of dealing with their institution. After today
they would be able to add one more. She turned her
screen so II could see everything she typed. She began
asking all those bank type questions while she entered my

answers through the keyboard. Then came the all important question, the sixty-four thousand dollar one. Banks like to know what you're going to invest their money in.

"Purpose of the loan?" Now she had turned to look at me.

II hesitated. Loan managers seem to know by looking at you if you're telling the truth. Should II give her the truth? "SRS plastic surgery," II answered.

"What type of surgery would that be?"

"A sex change."

"Now you're putting me on, right?"

"No! That's what II need to have done. II'm investing in me?"

"Are you going to become a man?"

"Heavens no! Right now II'm only half of a woman."

She was really having a difficult time holding back her amusement, and II was having as much trouble holding back my grin.

"Do you really want me to put that on the application?"

"Sure."

"Well, there's a first time for everything."

As she sent the file through electronically, we both felt free to have a good laugh, and as we waited, we talked about the changes II was making in my life. With the speed of computers the loan came back approved almost instantly. Obviously computers can't fathom what a sex changes is. II imagine II was served up for supper conversation around the loan manager's dinner table that night.

The postscript to this episode had an ironic twist. As Janet, II had no credit rating at all, but apparently, when II sent the official name change papers into the bank, the computer scanned its files for all references to my male name. It then began changing all the files it found from my male name to my female one. One of the files it found was the joint account II used to have with my wife. Arbitrarily it changed the name on that file to Janet. This linked all of my wife's current assets and the assets II had left behind under my male name to Janet. The computer determined that because of my old history of loan repayments under my previous name, and the assets II had left behind, and the mortgage II had co-signed on behalf of my wife, Janet was a good credit risk for this loan. II only found this out after the final loan papers indicating my net worth were mailed a few days later. Aren't computers efficient and wonderfully dumb machines?

All II had to do was complete the questions on the forms, mail the doctors' reports and laboratory test results, and send my deposit for the surgery. The physical tests, heart examinations and blood work all gave me a clean bill of health, with normal cholesterol levels and normal E.C.G. Maybe it was my lowered stress level now that my secret didn't scare me any more, or maybe it was all the exercise from walking everywhere that had improved my health, or maybe my heart had been miraculously healed. Only God has the answer to that mystery.

The two psychiatrist reports recommended the need for reconstructive surgery and confirmed to the clinic that I fully understood the implications this surgery would have in my life. The endocrinologist was the last to send in his report concerning my physical health and the hormonal treatment plan. By mid January everything had already been submitted, and II had received confirmation from the clinic that all was in order. They had scheduled my surgery for May thirteenth. There was only one slight problem. II had to loose twenty pounds before my surgery.

II was so excited that day, but II didn't have anyone to share my excitement with. Christmas that year was the first time in thirty-three years that II spent the holiday without the family. This was when II truly realized all the great family traditions that II had built with my family over a lifetime. It was also an opportunity to begin a whole new set of traditions. II made up my mind that II would not be a downcast by telling myself, "Poor me, II'm all alone for Christmas." Instead II offered to volunteer at the drop-in-center, to cook and serve on Christmas day. Then II tried to make my apartment as festive as possible by decorating my corn plant with a red bow, slices of apple dipped in cinnamon, and orange slices. It was a unique and great looking Christmas tree.

164

On Christmas day there was a layer of snow that made the magic of Christmas come alive. II got myself dressed up, put on my boots and winter coat, and walked downtown to the drop-in center. By the time II arrived, there were already people there from the street enjoying coffee and donated sweet treats. II donned my apron and set to work preparing and serving a full turkey dinner. As II worked and talked with the people, most of whom II already knew, II realized there was a reason for me to be there that day. II had once been where most of them were. Like me they had no family, no money, no food, and little hope. They were hurting in their spirits, hurting so deeply that I couldn't begin to imagine. The children were excitedly running about, playing with imaginary toys, waiting for a visit from Santa to bring a few gifts.

There was a lesson that day for me. We are all poor, no matter how much we might have. If we don't share what we are blessed with, our faith, hope and love, then we are destitute. II thought of my own family, enjoying what to these people would have been an unimaginable abundance. That was the most blessed Christmas II ever experienced. II was fortunate to experience the true meaning of Christmas and the opportunity to love people without expectations.

Shortly before Valentine's day, II called my daughter to tell her that II had a special Valentine's gift for her and to ask if there was some way she could come and pick it up. She had this thing about cows in decorating her apartment. II had made a pendulum clock in the shape of a cow, with the udders attached to the pendulum, causing them to swing back and forth. This opened the opportunity for us to see one another again. At first it was a short visit, and then she asked to come by a few days later. We sat and talked about our lives, and it was a wonderful reunion after so many months of separation. There was for the first time in our relationship a real openness, an opportunity for each of us to express our feelings, emotions and love for one another. We discovered that we were more alike than either of us thought. Each of us had been trying to keep our own secrets safe and secure from each other, trying to resolve our differences based on assumptions that we had made about one another.

A few weeks later she came for supper, and again we spent the whole night just talking about our lives. II came to know my daughter and her struggles. Without this opportunity II may never have gotten to know how special she is. More father-daughter bonding occurred in those six hours than in the previous twenty-six years that we had known one another, or II should say, in the twenty-six years that we thought we had known one another. Among other things, we discussed my desire for the surgery, and to my surprise she didn't object. We promised that we would never again need to hold secrets from each other. After she left, II wept for hours, having come to the realization that in those six hours God had again given me the desires of my heart.

The weeks developed into months as we rebuilt our relationship, talking daily on the phone. Neither of us wanted to miss anything that happened in the other's life. Through the restoration of my relationship with my daughter, my relationship with my grandson was restored also. II knew only God could have restored the family II loved.

Before II had the opportunity to see my grandson again after nearly four years, II wondered if he would re-member me. My physical appearance had changed dras-tically since the last time we had seen one another at that Easter dinner. At first he didn't recognize me, but as soon as II called his name, he remembered my voice. All his short life II was known as 'Poppy' to him, and to my daughter II will always be 'Dad'. During one of my daughter's visits, II asked her if she would prefer me to assume the role of Dad or Janet. Her answer shocked me. "Janet," she said, "I like you better."

This profusion of names for one person sometimes cre-ated confusion and humour. One night II invited my daughter and her girlfriend to a restaurant for supper. The waitress was standing at the end of our table wait-ing for us to make up our minds and place our order. My daughter turned to me and asked,

"Well, Dad, what're you having?"

The waitress had this puzzled look. Then my daughter realized what she had just asked, and her hand covered her mouth. Then the chuckles began. II sensed the waitress wasn't quite sure what to do. She seemed uneasy. It was my move to ease the tension.

"II guess II'd better start with a voice change."

That was what we needed, the freedom to laugh at a funny situation.

Soon it was May. II was busily scurrying around making all the final preparations for my trip, house cleaning, rug shampooing, painting and shopping. My goodness, you'd think II was having a baby with all the preparations II was making. II wanted everything ready for my return. It wouldn't be possible to do much heavy work for a while after II came home.

It was time to report my weight loss to the clinic, and II was fearful my surgery would be canceled. II hadn't lost all the weight they had requested. Should II lie about my weight? No! II couldn't go there anymore. No more lies. No more deceit. What should my reaction be if II was refused? II didn't feel that II could mentally withstand a postponement. II was convinced my decision would be clear. It had to be the operation or else. When II reported my weight to the surgeon at the clinic, II was pleasantly surprised. "That's great, Janet," he said. "We'll see you on the ninth as scheduled."

For a little over a year my apartment had become known as Aunt Janet's to the psychiatric and gay communities in the city. It was a safe house for people expe-

168

riencing crisis in their lives, a place where they could be consoled, confirmed they were loved and cared for without resorting to a hospital setting. It seemed a small service for me to offer in return for the many blessings others had showered on me in my times of need, so when II was to be out of town for the next two weeks, my twisted sense of humor kicked in, and II left the following message on my answering machine:

"Hi. . . Sorry, Aunt Janet's will be closed for the next two weeks due to major plumbing renovations."

12
It's Now Or Never

One of the advantages of all the traveling II did in my work was the accumulation of air miles with the airline II normally flew on. For some reason, during the time II was accumulating these air mile points II never used them. When II was trying to decide on the cheapest way to get to Montreal, II remembered the air miles II had accumulated. With a forty-five cent stamp II was able to send an official name change form to the airline, and within a week Janet was in possession of more than enough air mile points to get to Montreal for free.

II was up early the morning of the ninth. There were a lot of last minute preparations to finish, and II was in a hyper state of excitement, but first II needed to calm my spirit in prayer.

II had purchased two new outfits the week before, especially for my trip. These outfits had a symbolic meaning that would probably only make sense to me. They represented the transitions II was making. One consisted of a dress pair of slacks and a top for the trip to Montreal, the other a skirt and top for the trip home. Today was the start of a whole new life. The old would soon pass away.

At eleven forty-five that morning the airport transportation van pulled up in front of the apartment building door right on time. Once II was in the van, it was just another ride to the airport, and shortly II was fast asleep. II don't even remember leaving the city. It seemed as though II had just closed my eyes when they were waking me up in front of the terminal. Once inside II made straight for the check-in counter. While II was standing there waiting for the attendant to finish with the man in front of me, another man came running up and pushed his way ahead of me.

"Sorry, but I'm late," he said, out of breath.

The clerk, who was just finished with the person before me, rebuffed him.

"Sir, this lady is next. You'll have to wait your turn."

II felt smug hearing those special words, "this lady".

"Oh, it's okay. This is the beginning of my new life, and II have plenty of time left," II said with a smile.

As II approached the clerk, he said,

"You know, not many people will do that these days."

"Well, II've waited a lifetime for this flight," I said. "A few more minutes won't matter."

Finally the boarding call came for Flight 414 to Montreal. It reminded me of the other time, in Halifax, when II was ready to board a flight to Montreal bound for England. This time there were no second thoughts, no tears.

172

II was ready. II was so relaxed about the whole trip that II fell asleep again almost as soon as II sat in my seat. II missed the thrill of the whole plane ride, listening to the rev of the engines, the acceleration down the runway, and then the last mighty thrust as the nose of the plane pointed skyward. II also missed lunch and had to be awakened when we were making our final descent into Montreal.

"Miss," said the stewardess. "We'll be landing in Montreal in a few minutes."

II was like a first time flyer, watching out the window as we descended on the city located at the end of my yellow brick road. II couldn't have been more excited when we touched down and experienced that sudden jolt and the roar of the reversed engines, just as if it had been the very first time. II had flown in and out of Montreal on many occasions, but today, oh, it was different. It was like II was on the good ship lollipop. After so many years of dreaming, scheming, lying and deceiving, II was finally going to be freed from my closet prison. Once in the terminal II made straight for the baggage area, picked up my luggage and went to one of the pay phones to dial the number II had been given.

"Hello, this is Janet Manne."

The voice on the other end greeted me in a French.

"Anglais, si vous plais."

"Welcome to Montreal, Janet. Place your luggage on a cart and proceed through the doors in front of you.

You'll be greeted by our driver. His name is Henri, parked immediately in front of the door."

Waiting there for me was a black limo and a driver with cap and white gloves.

"Bonjour, Janet," he said, and then he assisted me into the car and loaded my luggage into the trunk. II felt oh so special. II hadn't been expecting anything like this.

As we traveled through the city, the driver made me feel welcome in his city as he pointed out the landmarks and special points of interest. II didn't have the heart to tell him that II was very familiar with the city. II just wanted to soak up everything that was offered. The drive to the residence wasn't that long, and we seemed to be there in no time at all. The residence was located in a lovely residential neighborhood. In the driveway he came around and opened my door and extended his hand to help me out of the car. II waited as he retrieved my luggage, and then he escorted me to the door where II was greeted in French by the house mother and with a welcoming hug by the house nurse.

II gazed around the residence from the front foyer. It seemed so large and beautiful. For the next couple of weeks this was going to be my fairy tale castle, where all my dreams would come true. The house mother took me to my room at the top of the stairs and introduced me to my roommate, who was lying on her bed reading.

"Janet, this is Jackie. Jackie's from Oregon."

174

"Jackie, Janet is the first Canadian we've had here in three years."

"Hi, Sis," she said.

Jackie, II soon learned, had a great sense of humor. She was excited to go through my suitcase and help unpack it. "Now that we're sisters," she said, "I just wanted to see what I could borrow."

Once II was unpacked, she took me on a tour of the house and introduced me to the only male in residence, our own french chef, white top hat, white jacket, and everything. The size of the house surprised me. II had no idea that it could house so many people. She took me around the building, past the in-ground pool and patio and into the living room with its large fireplace and floor to ceiling windows. She began introducing me to the others in residence. Four of the girls had been though their surgery two weeks ago and were preparing to leave for home the next day. When they left, four other girls would be arriving from the hospital after they had their surgery. Then Jackie and II would be off for our operations, along with Julie and Kendra, who had not yet arrived. It was wonderful to meet so many people like me gathered in one house. After all, II had only met one or two others in my life.

We sat around getting to know one another and talking about our lives. It seemed like we were septuplets, seven peas from the same pod. Our ages ranged from thirty-six to fifty-six, and II seemed to be the grandmother of the group. Most were in their early forties. All but Julie had been married, and some more than once. Julie, however, was planning to be married in a couple of months and was accompanied by her fiancé. All of us who had been married at one time had children, and as a result of our choices we had all lost our family relationships. Some had been in their transition for as long as five years. II counted myself lucky to have only been in a state of flux for a little over a year. Most if not all had experienced severe depression, rejection, anger and most of all guilt. II mentioned how II had tossed everything from my past, the photos and mementoes, in the garbage. One by one the other girls said they too had done the same thing. One thing we could all agree on was the need to make that basic decision about who we were. With everything stripped away, we needed to lay our souls bare to ourselves. We could no longer lie to ourselves. When we were totally truthful, we all found that in reality we only had two choices, and we had all chosen to live.

Later that night Kendra arrived from Florida with her ex-wife. II thought how nice to have that special kind of relationship. Kendra and her ex-wife had been married for thirty-two years and felt they had such a great marriage and friendship that, when Kendra's secret came out, they decided not to throw away a beautiful friendship.

Our meals were anything but hospital or group home

fare. Every meal was a gourmet delight. Breakfast was à la carte. We simply told the chef what we would fancy, and he prepared it exquisitely, giving it his own special twist of excellence and presentation. The whole experience was like special treatment at an exclusive spa. The next day the four of us who would be operated on the following week met with the surgeon for the first time. We were interviewed separately and given an explanation of the procedures that would be taking place over the next few days with the opportunity to ask any questions we might have. Later that afternoon we met our other sisters as they returned to residence from the hospital. At dinner that night we noticed their discomfort by the way they tried to sit at the dining room table on their little inflatable doughnut rings. The next day we were treated to an escorted tour of the city in our chauffeured limousine. Most of our time in residence was spent talking about our families and children and our hopes and aspirations for our new lives when all this was over. Before meals there was the opportunity to walk the parkland trail along the river and to spend some quiet time appreciating the beauty of the emerging spring. Somehow it seemed to parallel what was taking place in our lives.

Sunday morning II was up at the crack of dawn. II put a pot of coffee on and spent some quiet time before the others started moving about. When the coffee was ready, II took Jackie a cup, and then II went out on the covered patio where II could reflect on where my life had

177

been and how different II expected my life was going to be when II returned home. In a mere thirty hours or less my life would be so changed forever, and II wanted to savor the miracle of the healing the Lord was permitting in my life. As I sat there and began to communicate with the Lord by simply being quiet and peaceful, II sensed again that still small voice within me, the one II had heard so many times since I learned to be quiet and listen.

"Peace, fear not. II have heard your cries."

It was a beautiful May morning, and II was soon joined by a few of the other girls and the chef who had come out to take our orders for breakfast. That particular Sunday was a special day. It was Mothers' day, of all days, and we were entering our final stages of preparation to become females.

After breakfast it was time to begin our day of preparation. Julie and II were being operated on the next day, Kendra and Jackie the day following. We had to remove all hair from below our necks to our ankles. Then we were inspected by the house mother and the house nurse. If either of them found a hair, we had to do it all over again until we passed to their satisfaction. After passing the tests we spent the rest of the morning assuring one another and spending time in solitude.

After lunch we began our preparations in earnest, taking the dreaded enemas and packing what we would need at the hospital. The rest of the afternoon we simply relaxed until it was time for a very light supper, after which we were driven to the hospital, only five minutes away from residence. It became evident that nothing we ate or did had been without reason. All of our meals were designed to assist in cleaning out our bowels. Every opportunity to talk with one another was designed to build confidence and assurance. The clinic's procedures were so well designed that everything moved smoothly without tension or stress.

After supper Julie and II were taken to the special twenty bed hospital that specialized in plastic surgery, around the corner from a large metropolitan general hospital. Once we had signed our lives away with all the forms and paper work, the nurses again inspected us for any signs of hair and then gave us the old enema trick again. With all the formalities over, we enjoyed a snack of juice and a cookie, and then it was time for sleep. II was so relaxed and confident in my decision that II drifted off to sleep and slept all night. II had to be awakened by the nurse in the morning.

The day of our anticipation finally dawned, and we were encouraged to get up and shower before signing our final forms and being visited by the surgeon and the anaesthetist. II suppose it was our last chance to halt the process if we had any remaining doubts. After we received a tranquilizer shot in the hip, Julie was wheeled out and taken for her surgery. As II lay there, a warm fuzzy feeling came over me, and II slowly drifted off into a peaceful sleep.

When II woke up the next day, it was all over. II had been born again. II didn't feel much sensation of pain. II was no longer a trans-sexual, no longer just a woman. II was a female according to society's yardstick to distinguish between genders.

Wednesday the nurse came in and encouraged us to get out of bed and take a shower before we had a light breakfast. After breakfast they had us on the move, and II went to visit Kendra and Jackie to see how they were making out. As II went in their room Jackie was already sitting up and having a good laugh.

"Come here, you've got to see this."

She hoisted her nighty. There on her abdomen was tattooed in indelible marker, "Created in Canada". As II told you before, Jackie had a sense of humor. Just before they wheeled her away for her surgery, she had taped an American flag to her abdomen with the words, "Made in U.S.A."

The surgical team, it seems, also had a sense of humor.

"Where can we have a smoke?" she asked.

"II don't know, but we can't smoke in here," II answered.

"Well, let's go outside."

We unhooked ourselves from the catheter bags and put the plugs into the end of the tubes, then made our way out the front door of the hospital. As we stood on the front steps of the hospital, we suddenly realized we

180

were standing at a bus stop when a bus pulled up and discharged some passengers. There we stood with our short hospital gowns covering our fronts and our hospital housecoats covering our backsides, with our catheter tubes hanging down our legs. When we tried to retreat back in the front doors, they were locked. We hadn't realized that the doors would automatically lock behind us when we went out. For once Jackie was at a loss to see the humor in our situation.

For the next few days it seemed that the surgeons had also connected my tear ducts to my bladder. All anyone had to do was look at me, and II was a weeping idiot. II had become very weepy and emotional. II was happy, sad, lonely and afraid. Often II was all of these at the same time.

Before leaving the hospital that Friday, II had the nurses try and reach my daughter to let her know that everything was okay, but she couldn't be reached. When we arrived at the residence, we were greeted by the other girls and received our 'welcome home cocktail', a fifty-fifty combination of prune juice and mineral oil. Several times that afternoon II tried reaching my daughter, but there still was no answer. Since she had call display on her phone, II began to wonder and fear. Perhaps II had pushed her too far. Had she reached the limit of her acceptance of my choice? II was feeling desperately lonely and alone. Kendra had support from her ex-wife, Julie had her fiancé. The impact of suddenly feeling totally

181

alone in the world with absolutely no family made me feel like an orphan. That was until II went to my room. There on the headboard of my bed were two bouquets of flowers. One was from the clinic staff. The other had a card in a sealed envelope. Before opening the envelope II wondered who could possibly know where II was, since II hadn't given the name of the clinic or its whereabouts to anyone. II didn't want any outside interference. As II read the card, the tears rolled down my cheeks. II could barely read the message for the tears that filled my eyes.

Peace in Christ
Love
Your Family
Rainbow Community Church

Suddenly II felt loved. II felt ashamed. II felt joyful. II felt like II belonged somewhere because someone cared. II think my problem was wanting to hold on to the past while being a new creation, and then II began to appreciate the thoughtfulness and the trouble they had gone to locate the clinic, just to let me know II was loved by my family of choice.

The next day II stood in front of the floor length mirror in the bathroom and beheld the reflection of my new body in it's entirety for the first time. II was truly a member of the Rainbow family. II was black, blue, yellow, red, orange, green and every shade in between.

God's covenant with me was complete. He had painted a rainbow on my body.

II'd like to lie and tell you that the operation wasn't painful, but we all agreed that the pain we were experiencing for those few days couldn't measure up to the pain we had experienced for a lifetime.

The discomfort mainly came from our attempts to find a comfortable sitting position. Now it was our turn to battle with the little round inflatable rings that had plagued the girls the week before. The most comfortable position seemed to be a partial lying and partial sitting position. Then we would begin to roll from one cheek to the other like a cork bobbing on the water. The secret was in finding just the right amount of air in the doughnut to keep the sensitive area elevated while providing a cushion that didn't roll around when you sat on it. The other area of discomfort was mental. Almost all my life II had sat on the toilet like a female. Now, because of the catheter connected to my bladder, II had to stand like a man to empty my catheter tube.

Bright and early Monday morning the doctor came in and removed the dressings, packing and catheters. Then the house nurse came in and gave us instructions on the care of our new areas, baths to prevent infection, dilations to keep the skin in the newly constructed areas stretched. Jackie just couldn't resist nicknaming the dilators the "Three Amigos". Five times a day we went through a ritual of baths and dilations. This would be a daily pro-

183

cess for the next several months until the frequency could be tapered off.

Finally II reached my daughter. She had been away for the weekend at her friend's cottage. It sounded great just to talk with her and hear her voice, to receive her reassurance that everything was good between us.

II had a pastor friend in Montreal who had moved from the church II once attended. Every time II was in the area II made a point of reaching him to talk or of showing up at his church for Sunday services. It was hard for me to make my Sunday morning visits a surprise. II had the only white face in the congregation, and II stood out like a flourescent sign in the night. On Tuesday II gave him a call,

"Hi, yeah, it's me. II'm in Montreal again."

"Where are you? Why don't you come over for supper. Tonight's prayer meeting at the church."

"Well, II'd like to, but right now II'm just recovering from surgery."

Then II talked to him about my relationship with my wife. He already knew about our separation, but he didn't know any specific details of our breakup.

"What sort of surgery did you have that you had to come all the way to Montreal?"

II tried to break it to him gently, but there was no easy way.

"The reason we broke up was because II was a transsexual."

"What?"

"II believed myself to be a female, a woman, so II've just had reconstructive surgery to eliminate the problem that had been hanging around all my life."

"I wish we had talked about this sooner. I know we could have fixed the problem," he said.

II told him the problem was fixed now, and that II had sought a healing in so many ways that this was the last alternative guaranteed to create peace in my life. He regretted that he couldn't come to visit because he had serious reservations about my decision. A few weeks later II sent him a letter filling him in on the whole story. II haven't heard from him since.

The house mother shared with me that the girls in the front office had received a couple of impassioned calls from another person in Ontario desperately seeking assistance. This person, just like me, had been to the Clarke Gender Clinic and had also been refused feminization. II talked to the girls in the office and told them it was perfectly okay for them to give my name and telephone number to this person, and if the person wanted to contact me, II would help in any way II could. Unfortunately the Montreal clinic only provides the final solution to our problem. Unlike the United States, where there are many counseling and support clinics, in Canada we are limited to a few clinics similar to the Clarke. The problem is that when you are refused by these clinics, your life becomes hopeless, unless you have some other alternative to turn

185

to, such as II had.

Our final days as sisters were spent sharing our hopes and aspirations for the years ahead. Jackie had plans to begin a charter air service from Oregon into Canada. Julie and her fiancé were looking forward to their marriage in a couple of months. Kendra and her ex were returning to Florida to work together as contract nurses. II think we were all excited about returning home and getting on with our new lives. Did II feel different? II sure did, and II liked the feeling of being uniquely and wonderfully made. Did God have a hand in this? Perhaps. II'd like to think He did when II saw the rainbow on my body. Do II have any regrets? Yes, my greatest regret is the fact that II was put in a situation for whatever reason where it was necessary to make this choice at all. Other regrets also center on things over which II had no control, especially the family's choices about how they needed to deal with the situation.

The real cost of our transformation was cheap financially compared to the king's ransom it cost in emotions, family, friends, associates and careers. Now that this stage of our lives was complete, we simply wanted to return to society and live life as females.

Knowing what II do now, would II make the same choice or chosen suicide instead? II definitely wouldn't choose the path of suicide. Would II have chosen surgery sooner? Probably not, given that II had a responsibility for the needs of the family that outweighed my personal needs. Do II feel guilty about my choice and the impact on other people? No!

At one time II was upset that the Clarke Clinic's unexplained decision to exclude me from their program required me to underwrite the cost of my own surgery, while others were sent to England with the cost of their surgery covered by O.H.I.P. Now II rest in the knowledge that only the Lord knew the type of support II required, and He didn't have a sterile isolated hospital room for two weeks in England in mind for me. He knew that the sisterhood II would experience in Montreal would provide the healing balm I needed, that our ability to embrace, comfort, and shed tears with one another was a sure cure for the malady of my heart.

II was ready to go home, and unlike the other times II had traveled and found myself wishing that II didn't have to pack myself away in my closet when it was time to go home, this time II was excited about returning as a new person.

What a feeling of confidence II had as II entered the terminal for the first time dressed as a female in a long flowing skirt. My vanity and pride wouldn't allow me to carry my little red doughnut through the airport. It was safely out of sight in my luggage. II was like a first time flyer again, asking for the window seat, though II normally preferred the aisle seat where there is more room. II wasn't going to spend this flight sleeping. II wanted to savor every moment.

After II had taken my seat on the plane, I was soon joined by a young man about the age of my eldest son. II thought he must be very important since he was hardly in his seat before he was trying to set up his computer on his lap. Then he couldn't sit still. He bounced around, and II thought to myself, "What's his problem. Could his underwear be too tight?" II was waiting for him to start up a conversation, like most seat-mates do. His mannerisms and fidgeting were becoming very irritating. We had reached cruising altitude, and the stewardess came along offering us drinks and peanuts. Finally he stopped diddling with his computer.

"Hi," he said, "Do you live in Montreal?"

"No, II was born there last week."

He laughed. "You're kidding, right? This is some kind of put on."

"No, II just had a sex change operation two weeks ago."

The dumbfounded look on his face finished the conversation then and there. He packed up his computer and left his seat for the rest of the flight. Had II actually exploded this guy's mind at thirty-two thousand feet?

Finally after being jolted and bounced about in the airport limousine van, II was standing at the front door of my apartment building. It was then II realized that II was no longer the princess II had been in Montreal. There was no white gloved knight to help me as II struggled to move my luggage from the building door to my apartment. II was now required to pay the price for my vanity and pride. My body was in a total state of revolt. II hurt everywhere, and II felt that if I didn't soon get into my apartment my insides were likely to be laying on the floor.

Part IV

Hi, God!
Thank You.

13
You are God's Gift To You

When II reached my apartment door, II began rummaging through my purse, fumbling for the keys. II unlocked the door. All II could think of was dropping my bags inside the door and throwing myself on the bed in complete exhaustion.

"Welcome home, Dad."

As II swung the door open, my daughter's greeting was an unexpected yet completely welcome surprise. For a moment II was speechless, and then my eyeballs began to drown in the tears that spilled down my cheeks, moistening my lips with their salty flavor. II didn't notice the pain and discomfort that only seconds before had nearly made me collapse. We stood there embracing one another, our tears intermingled on our cheeks. Words would have been inappropriate and completely meaningless as father and daughter reunited now as two females.

Once the lump in my throat had partially cleared, II

was barely able to squeeze out a muted whisper through the tears.

"I love you. Just having you here is such a blessing, you know. For a while in Montreal II feared II lost you from my life again when II couldn't get you on the phone."

After we both stopped crying, she invited me into my own apartment.

"Come on, Dad. Supper's ready."

Following supper we just sat and talked for several hours about the events that had taken place in Montreal and the significance they would have in both of our lives, now that her dad was a female.

During the next six weeks while my body was healing, my daughter was a big help answering the myriad of girl type questions that my gender change brought into my life. These conversations opened a whole new level of openness in our communication and relationship.

During the healing period it was necessary for me to take baths a couple of times a day. Following each bath II had to dilate the reconstructed area to stretch and keep the transplanted tissue flexible. When II left the Montreal clinic they suggested that intercourse was possible after six weeks and was the best form of dilation, otherwise it was necessary to maintain a regular schedule of dilations for the next year. I'll bet the intercourse route would have been more pleasurable than a hard plastic dildo.

After a year II still experienced discomfort every time II went to the washroom. My family doctor referred me to a gynaecologist. Just the word gynaecologist seemed to confirm my complete transformation. II was being referred to an area of medicine that flashed a neon sign outside the doctors office, 'No Men Allowed'. Entering the doctor's office, II took a seat in the waiting room. Glancing around at my new environment, II noticed the room's walls were covered with snapshots of babies, sort of an Obs/Gyn trophy room, II suppose. As II sat there in the middle of all the mommies-to-be, the receptionist brought me a set of questionnaires to fill out, you know, the kind that ask for all that family data stuff. II was confronted by a whole series of very interesting and thought provoking questions. These were going to take some creative thought. Should II ignore them? Should II lie? Should II answer them as truthfully as I could? I answered them as truthfully as I dared, with tongue firmly in cheek. II couldn't help wondering if the smirk in my mind was evident on my face.

Are you pregnant? - No.
When was your last period? - I can't remember.
Did you experience difficulty with your periods? - No.
How many children do you have? - Five.
Did you have difficulty during pregnancy? - No.

195

When II returned the questionnaire to the nurse, she ushered me into an examination room and instructed me to remove my clothes from the waist down, put on the gown, and lie on the table with my feet in the stirrups. The doctor would be with me shortly. Could II have any further doubts that II was a female? A male would never be expected to assume such a submissive position.

"Well, what's the problem today?"

The doctor's broad smile accented the white teeth that shone like pearls against his dark complexion. II explained the discomfort that II felt when going to the washroom because of the raw area between the urethra and the clitoris. When he had completed his physical examination, he didn't appear overly concerned about my situation. Of course not. He wasn't experiencing the burning sensation every time he went to the washroom. He recommended the use of an estrogen cream that would heal the area within a short period of time but also double the amount of estrogen II was taking, perhaps producing stronger feelings and desires than II wanted or was ready to experience. II was unsure if this was the best course of action, but he explained that during his training in England he had gained some experience with trans-sexual surgery, and this made it easier for me to trust his judgment. The last thing II wanted to do was provide a training opportunity for yet another doctor to learn what made a trans-sexual tick. II had already trained four.

A couple of months after the operation, II reopened 'Aunt Janet's' and returned to volunteering with the psychiatric survivors, but this time II didn't feel the same sense of fulfillment. The group dynamics had changed. The members had become more abusive towards each other and were fighting amongst themselves. They had returned to selfishness, power struggles and squabbling. My mental health was at stake if II continued in such a hostile environment.

How could God call me to minister to these people? Had He in fact called me to this ministry, or was it of my own choosing? This was something II needed to clarify in my mind. As time went by it became more and more evident to me that volunteering like this was a way for me to feel needed while superficially ministering to people's needs. They didn't want to hear about God, and they didn't care about anything except when they'd receive their next government check or who'd loan them money and cigarettes. They were verbally abusive when II wouldn't give them what they wanted from the little resources that II did have. II felt guilty abandoning them to their own devices, but II had to come to the realization that some people prefer to live in their squalor and ignorance, rather than take the risk of accepting real help. My guilt caused feelings of despondency. II believed II had failed because II had nothing to offer them, but the last thing II needed was to allow myself to feel like a failure because of other people's sickness.

II could see that 'Aunt Janet's', while trying to help people in a positive way, was actually feeding their self centeredness, so II stopped volunteering, stopped using my apartment as a refuge, and stopped feeding them. II began looking for some other need, where God's calling for my life might be fruitful. The guilt and despondency created a feeling of emptiness in my life, especially when II couldn't get any answers from God to my question, "What should I do now?" When II called on Him, He always seemed to be out on the golf course.

My own sense of worth has always required that II have a project, a goal, a mark to shoot for. These were all absent now from my life, and so II believed that my life had lost its value. The emptiness in my life plus the completion of my greatest goal left me without a purpose and without the friends who II thought would support me through the difficult times. II was forced to ride out these storms of my depressive periods alone, since God was still on the heavenly golf course.

II had finally reached the pinnacle of life, II thought. II stood on top of the highest mountain in the world. Below me the entire earth was blanketed in the clouds as far as the east is from the west and the north from the south. The entire earth was as though it were invisible. II stood alone with my solitary completed dream. II had no more mountain to scale. Why was II so empty inside? My mood level had sunk below sea level. II had nothing to live for. Suicide felt again like my only answer. Fortunately my psychiatrist had been keeping a close eye on my mood swings, and he sensed my depression was getting out of control. Again II was committed to the Homewood hospital, for my own safety, at least until II was again able to cope with the fears II had about my future and the absence of a dream. He had expected something like this might happen. He had read a report prior to my operation that warned how approximately thirty percent of post operative trans-sexuals become suicidal for one reason or another following surgery.

When he mentioned this to me before my surgery, II wondered how anyone could be depressed after realizing the ultimate goal of their lives. What II didn't see coming was the effect of an anticlimax in my life. How could II become depressed when everything II had hoped for, dreamed of all my life, was now reality? Because it was over. The dream was fulfilled. What on earth was left? Surely II should be the happiest person alive. But, II wasn't. There was still a hole that wasn't filled.

In the realization of my dream II had directed all my energy into accomplishing one thing, and II hadn't taken the time to explore what my life would be like without my dream. Likewise, II was positive God wanted me to serve Him in a ministry of servanthood, but why was He leaving the area of service for me to decide? How unfair. II was uncomfortable with this freedom of choice. Was II to be another Moses, wandering around for years before II could find my ministry?

199

Sometimes people cross our path, and a door of opportunity opens, permitting a different direction or confirming previously held convictions. Such was the case one Sunday evening when the pastor of the Rainbow church began his message.

"Who you are is God's gift to you," he said. "What you do with it is your gift to God."

He said this not once but several times. It was like God's spirit was blocking out the rest of the pastor's message that evening as my mind became transfixed by this one statement. Finally, God's golf game was over, II thought. Perhaps II can get some direction now. It was like He was sitting there beside me, nailing this message into my spirit. It confirmed everything that II believed was His will for my life, but like always, the way II would serve was still left up to me to choose.

Falling from my mountain top experience, II had tumbled into the valley where II lay broken, bruised and feeling sorry for myself, because II no longer had a significant dream. After indulging myself in a pity party, it was time to get started all over again.

Meanwhile, God was still trying to get my attention through the ministry of the Rainbow church. There were still many areas of anger, pain and rejection that needed to be dealt with in my life as II clawed and crawled my way back up the mountain.

II was feeling used by the psychiatric community. They only needed me for what II was able to give. When

200

II pulled the plug on my giving, they pulled the rug out from under me. Again II was alone except for the people of the Rainbow church. Meeting together once each week on Sundays provided little opportunity for interaction with the other people of the church. Although we shared a common belief in Christ, a need for prayer and corporate worship, II felt isolated, perhaps because II was so much older or because our social interests weren't compatible.

The months that followed were lonely, but by now II should have been accustomed to aloneness. There was a need in the new me to break the patterns of the past. II needed to thaw out the feelings of intimacy that II had kept in the deep freeze for so long. As II looked at the small church family community where II felt safe and acceptable, II felt excluded from intimacy with any of the females because II was a heterosexual female, and the guys weren't interested in me socially because II was't one of them. At the time II might have been comfortable in a lesbian relationship, but at the same time II felt that it wouldn't satisfy my deepest desires. II really didn't know what was right, but emotionally II ached to be wanted, to be needed, to be held close to another human being.

One Sunday night a fellow entered my life as a friend. Over the next several weeks we spent time together over lunch and coffee. At first it made me feel good finally to be in public as a couple, although II knew he might be gay. He wanted moral support as he began to emerge from his closet. He had confided in his son about his sexual confusion but not his common law wife of eleven years. Instantly II identified with his pain. II had been there, bought the t-shirt, and sent the post card.

As II listened to him, II relived my lies and deceit. While we met together, his wife thought he was attending Bible study at the church. II encouraged him to tell her the truth about the other side of his life. He promised he would, but never did.

Somehow he had convinced the social services people that he was in a physically abusive relationship and needed their help to escape. His wife was the sole support for their family, and so he also needed their support in housing and finance. Within weeks social services had provided everything he needed. They jumped him to the head of the waiting list for subsidized housing, all because of the alleged abuse. While he waited to make his exit, he spent the time dividing their possessions right down to the salt and pepper in the boxes. He had taken inventory and knew exactly what and where everything was, so that on the day he was to leave he could quickly pack his car and his friend's truck as soon as his wife left for work.

II wasn't comfortable with the choices he was making, but then it wasn't my life, and yet II felt that II was being his accomplice through my silence.

The day he moved II offered to help put things into

his new apartment, but he declined my help, fearing that people in his new building might think he was gay because of his association with me. What he didn't know was that II already knew many of the people in the building, though this was something he would soon discover.

A few weeks after he was settled in, he invited me for dinner one evening. He was still ashamed of me, II guess, because he provided me with a key a couple of nights before so I could let myself into the building and avoid the door buzzer.

II don't follow instructions very well. You might even say II ignore them, especially when someone says indirectly that they are ashamed to be seen with me. That evening II left his door key at home. When II arrived at the main door to his building, II engaged in conversation with a couple of the residents II knew and told them that II had been invited to Ray's for dinner. II knew that it would feed the rumor mill, at least for a couple of days.

II rang his door buzzer while II talked to the ladies, forcing him to confirm over the intercom that I was in fact visiting his apartment. My public announcement was solely for the benefit of the ladies. He sounded surprised, no, II think it was shock, when II said good night to the ladies by name and then asked him to push the button since II had forgotten my key. After supper, on my way out, he did walk me part of the way down the hall to where the doors of the games room were open and many of the residents were playing cards. As II stood for a moment in the open doors, II called a greeting to those playing cards. Once II had their attention, II then turned and shouted down the hall, "Good night, Ray."

II'm not going to allow anyone to make me less than who II am. They can't have that power over my life any more.

II have God's gift. II am who II am.

14
My Gift

What's wrong with this picture? All my life II thought II was a giving person, just like my dad and his father before him. Was II only giving out of my abundance? Was that why God wasn't particularly interested in me? For most of my life that was true, but after II left my closet, II was forced to give out of my poverty, not just to God, but to everyone.

The evening II appropriated the pastor's message into my life, II mistakenly placed the emphasis on the last part of the statement, "What you do with your gift is your gift to God." II had placed such an emphasis on trying to accomplish this that II hadn't really come to the realization of just what my gift from God was.

My uniqueness had really been there all the time. II was about to discover that my gift was not because of how my life has been altered through a set of circumstances, but because II'm exactly the way God created me. II am who II am (Exodus 3:14).

A very dear friend in my life called me up short on this. "You're problem isn't that you can't give," she said. "It's that you refuse to receive. That makes you selfish. You want to give, give, give, but you refuse to allow me the opportunity to give back to you. How do you expect God to minister to you through me or anyone else? How do you expect Him to answer your prayers when you exclude other people from giving?"

Since II didn't have unique or special talents or abilities, II had to give, or else II didn't believe II was able to please God. In short, II was trying to work for my salvation, though II knew in my mind that Jesus had already bought it. II was disappointed to realize that God really didn't need my help to accomplish anything. He appreciated my help when II was obedient to His leading, but if II wasn't, He'd get the job done without me.

While volunteering with the psychiatric survivors, II stood watching a man slip and slide as he inched his way along the icy sidewalk. Almost in front of our building his feet went out from under him, and he looked a bit like Bambi on all fours before he crashed onto the sidewalk. II responded by flying out the door with little forethought. Within three steps II was sliding across the ice covered walk on my bum before we came together in a pile of twisted humanity. Slowly we helped each other get to our feet and limp our way into the office. That's how I met my friend Bill.

Bill lives with voices and visions in his brain that are rarely silent. He's a schizophrenic. Bill also listens to another voice, the Holy Spirit. Bill distinguishes himself as being set apart because of his faith in God. Despite the turbulence in his brain, he has a gentleness and peace surrounding his life that makes being his friend special. His greatest pleasure in daily life is obtained from the rugs he creates for shows, display and gifts. The receipt of a card of thanks, a kiss on the cheek, or the opportunity to show his scrap book of photos and ribbons makes his face beam from within.

As II walked to volunteer with the psychiatric survivors, II would pass the home where Bill has lived for the past nineteen years. When he was sitting outside II'd stop and talk, and slowly our friendship grew to include other residents of the home. Eventually the administrator asked if II would be interested in volunteering my time to organize activities for the residents. By this time II was no longer volunteering with the psychiatric survivors, and this invitation seemed to be a door that God was opening for me. Everything II was learning about my unique gift flew out the window when II became caught up with these people. Soon II was roaring down the same old dusty road with my wheels stuck in the same old ruts.

The residence where these people lived was disgusting. It was a fire trap too. II thought of it as a modern day dungeon to house psychiatric survivors, a place where the unwanted and destitute were hidden from view in our affluent city. II was disgusted and became a quasi social activist with the local health inspectors, social services and fire department. These agencies weren't interested,

207

and if they weren't, who would be? Me? II tried, but II fear profits have a louder voice than fairness, dignity and do-gooders like me.

It cost these residents every cent they received in subsidy and pension for their room and board to live in these deplorable and degrading conditions. One night, for dinner, their meal consisted of roast chicken backs and vegetables. Chicken backs are famous for their skin, bone, gristle and minimal protein.

The nursing staff were lackadaisical in their duties and at best poorly trained. They didn't practice sterile techniques when changing residents' dressings and probably perpetuated the infections that never seemed to heal. What little finances the residents had for personal needs were quicky gobbled up by the residence operator, who charged for any health care item not covered by the government.

The cook was once reprimanded for overspending the eight hundred dollar food budget he had to feed forty people three times a day. That's only sixty cents per person per day for food. For heaven's sake, it costs me fifty-one cents a day to feed my cat. The more time II spent at the residence, the more abuse II watched, until II couldn't tolerate it any longer. II left.

Bill and a couple of the other residents invited me to their bi-weekly Happy Handicaps social outing, held at Bill's church. Through this group II came into contact with Bill's pastor. Bill often spoke about his church and

208

his relationship with Jesus, and he was eager for me to attend church with him. It was difficult to keep putting him off, but frankly II was scared to death to go to a Baptist church again. II had begun to feel that Baptists all held judgmental attitudes, which meant rejection and pain for me. II had already experienced that type of Christianity, thank you very much, and II preferred to stay at the Rainbow church.

While II loved God, II feared the people who made up His church. For twenty some years II had been indoctrinated with fundamental Christian teaching that strongly promoted the idea of "loving the sinner and hating the sin". Sounds like a good policy, but you've immediately set yourself up to be the judge. If you're comfortable with that, go ahead, but II think it stinks. It develops into a graduated scale of sin. Then every thought, word and action must be placed on the scale and compared to the bias of each group.

That's not what I understand the Bible to say. Sin is sin. It doesn't come in shades or degrees.

The Christian church throughout the ages has been developing this scale and wielding it quite abusively, ousting individuals and groups according to its sacred definition of right and wrong.

One night at the Happy Handicaps, Bill's pastor came over and introduced himself to me. II don't know what came over me, but II asked if he had a couple of minutes to talk. In his office II explained about myself and that

209

II had gone through a sex change. II asked if he would be uncomfortable if II came to his church services, and II asked him to run it by the deacons' board as well. II didn't want to create a problem for myself or make other people uncomfortable by my presence. Two weeks later the pastor came over and invited me to attend their worship services whenever II wanted to come. No longer did II have an excuse. Bill and II attended the next Sunday. A good thing too, II was almost running out of excuses.

As we approached the open front doors of the church, II could see two men just inside the door greeting people as they arrived. II was hoping II could just sneak past them without being seen. Well, II didn't succeed.

"Morning, Bill," said this one fellow with a brush cut.

As I tried to hide behind Bill and sneak around behind him, I noticed an outstretched hand.

"Good morning. My name is Roy, and you are?"

II had been caught.

"Good morning. My name is Janet," II answered softly. Now II figured he knew everything about me and my past. After all, my voice was a dead give away.

Roy didn't appear shocked or surprised by the discrepancy between my voice and my appearance. Instead he took me to the guest book at the side of the stairs and gave me a stick-on yellow rose for my blouse. This is like pinning a target on your back and walking in the country during deer hunting season. It's a neon sign that flashes,

"I'm new." Meanwhile, II guess Bill had forgotten that II was with him and had taken his seat in the sanctuary. As II made my way to him, II met so many nice people. II was actually pleased that II had this neon sign announcing to everyone that II was a visitor to their congregation. Now I saw what II would have been missing if II had obeyed that inner voice of my fear and bias.

Within the next week II received a nice note from one of the female pastors welcoming me and inviting me to attend their services on a regular basis. Along with the teaching that II enjoyed at the Rainbow church and with Father John, my personal Christian growth at this new church was now challenging many of my misinterpreted fundamental beliefs. Had II been successful that Sunday morning at slipping in and out of the church without being noticed, like many people, for watever personal reasons they may have, II'm convinced the Lord would never have had the opportunity to bless my life the way it has been blessed.

It was a drastic contrast to what II had experienced when II once attended a church located right across the street from a hotel in New Brunswick. II had chosen to go to that particular church because of the sign on their front lawn - "Moncton's Friendliest Church". It turned out to be a lesson in what not to do if you're bold enough to proclaim your friendliness. As they say on the east coast, "That was some bad Sunday morning worship service." When I entered the church, no one

211

greeted me, no one offered me an order of service, and apparently the pew I sat in belonged to the people who came and glowered at me before finally sitting somewhere else. After the service II think the minister retreated out the back door, because he was no where to be seen. That Sunday morning II spoke to no one.

II was pleased to see on my next trip to Moncton that their latent friendliness had been awakened by a letter they received shortly after my first visit.

II must admit that, as a complete stranger entering a church for the first time, II'm usually entering with a degree of fear and apprehension of judgment, but that's my insecurity. II've been told that the rules for membership in God's kingdom are actually different from the rules for membership in the local church. The local church's rules are more stringent concerning membership. II guess this means, well, II don't know what it means. Perhaps God's rules are too lax.

There's an irony here. The Christian church expends a great deal of effort and time following Christ's command to go into all the world preaching His gospel and making disciples. Yet all too many times when the world appears at the door, it is screened by some unspoken set of values. "This one's a keeper," the church says, "but these other two need to be thrown back." There are many disenfranchised people, Christians and non-Christians both, who are thrown back by church communities that have exchanged the good news of the gospel for their own set of rules and commandments.

Why has the church turned the simplicity of Christ's teaching into a gospel of enslavement? This is bondage, a bondage based on the idea that above all God wants all people to be healthy, wealthy and wise, and all they need to do is send in their seed money. When this seed money is planted, it will sprout a hundred fold increase in their finances by opening the flood gates of heaven.

What happened to the commandments Jesus left for us? Why do we choose to ignore them? Why are we trying to reinvent what Christ accomplished at the cross? Wake up Christians! We are hypocrites! We teach our children the simple truth of God's love, and by the time they reach their teens we have piled on so many expectations of our own that they can no longer see Jesus. What they do see is our hypocrisy, and they turn their backs. Mine did, and II'm afraid that because of our estrangement II may never be able to right the wrongs II've created.

The Lord has given me a new chance at life and a gift of uniqueness. How should II offer this to Him? II don't have a nice pat answer. Life is not the accomplishments we achieve but the journey we experience along the way. Most of my life has been filled with valleys and mountain tops, but that's not who II am or ever have been. II'm a traveler, sometimes alone and sometimes in great crowds. II'm beginning to learn that II've never been alone. Jesus has always been with me, even when II didn't want him there. There have been and continue to be people who love and care for me, who disciple me. There is nothing that I could ever give to God, or do for God, that could repay these gifts.

What then should my gift be?

Father, II know that II've done things II shouldn't have and not done things II should have. Please forgive me. Your Son, Jesus, died for me on the cross, and you lifted Him from the dead so that II could come to you just as II am. II want your Son to dwell in me and be Lord and Savior of my life.

This is my humble gift, me, everything II have.

15
It's me, Lord

Week after week Bill and II worshiped at his church. II was becoming so comfortable in their midst that II was beginning to forget about the process of change II had come through, but slowly my old enemy, doubt, crept back into my thought life. Why were they being so nice to me? They must be hoping that II'd soon realize II didn't belong there and just leave of my own accord. They probably thought II was queer, strange or funny, just humoring me. Doubt had been an enemy of mine for years. It took the truth and twisted it into a two edged weapon of self abasement and criticism. It made me wary of people who were nice to me. It was all the excuse II needed to keep people at bay and distance myself from close emotional encounters.

Overcoming my enemy meant lowering my guards and defense mechanisms. In other words, II had to allow myself to become vulnerable, but as the weeks went by these people weren't changing their acceptance of me. II began to feel that perhaps they really were for real, so II decided to risk that they were, and II began removing my protective walls.

II'm not sure how many of these people actually knew about my past or even cared. You see, there's a great myth when you're afraid of being different, the myth that everyone cares about your diffrences as much as you do. Now, really and truly, how many people really care deeply that you have a wart on the end of your nose, besides you, that is. II was so sure that my deep voice had caused most people to put two and two together and realize what I was, but most of them probably didn't know or care.

The adult Sunday school class at one point decided that they should study the plight of disenfranchised Christians, people like me, anyone who didn't fall into the heterosexual stereotype. They were looking to discover how they might overcome the mistakes that the Christian church had made in the past, mistakes that had so left many people, both Christians and non-Christians alike, alienated from the church. Their concern was how to take the message of the gospel of Christ to a disinterested and fearful people who had already been rejected by the church.

II sat in on the session pertaining to the gay and lesbian community. As II looked around the room, II wondered, "Are there any gay or lesbian people even present?" Of course there weren't. Everyone there was heterosexual, middle aged or seniors. How could a serious discussion take place without those who had been disenfranchised? How would these church people learn what it was like to be disenfranchised? It soon became apparent that some class members had done a little reading about the spiritual issues facing the gay community, but their knowledge lacked any appreciation for the feelings of being ostracized. Being ostracized as a gay person is similar to any form of ostracization, but it also carries with it the stigma of being queer and outside the will of God.

It wasn't long before the standard Christian cliche had been expressed – "We must love the sinner and not the sin." Now II had promised the pastor that II would remain silent during this class, but of all statements that might have been made, this one moved me to my feet like no other. II couldn't remain silent and let people believe that it's possible to divide, segment and separate people like dissecting a frog into the pieces we can tolerate and those we can't. It's true that we don't have to condone wrong behaviour (Careful! This implies a judgment according to our own standards), but when we decide to love a person the way Christ loves us, we better be prepared to follow His example and love the whole person, and folks, sometimes this isn't easy.

Once on my feet II became oblivious to my deep voice and the number of people in the class. II began by announcing to the group that II had been a trans-sexual but that now II was a female. If there had been any doubt in anyone's mind before that morning, it had been dispensed with by my admission. Then II went on to ex-

217

plain that II am a whole person, that II'm not divisible, and that like many people II have come to Christ with past baggage. I tried to make them understand that if they truly wished to reach out to disenfranchised people, they would have to do away with their pigeonhole mentality and begin loving others for who they are.

Just having the confidence to stand before these people and admit my warts took a great load of concern from my shoulders. After that morning session they would either outright reject me or continue to tolerate me. Their continued acceptance enabled me to feel a new found sense of freedom in my life. To my surprise a number of people approached me following that class and during the following weeks to express their appreciation for my openness, and to thank me on behalf of their family members who had been disenfranchised from the church because of life styles that had been judged contrary to accepted beliefs. II can't help wonder where II would be today in my walk with Christ had the people in that Sunday school class and the others in Bill's church decided that "II wasn't a keeper" and had thrown me back into the pond of the disenfranchised.

Imagine if you will, Janet the tax collector, sitting all day long in her toll booth beside the road into town, collecting a toll from all who enter into the city. To each toll she adds a small surcharge for her personal debt reduction, which nets a tidy profit for herself. When Jesus spots her, He calls out to her.

"Hi, Janet. I'm looking for people to follow me, and you look like you'd be a good candidate, but it's too bad you had a sex change, and you're probably gay besides. Most of your kind are. I'll tell you what. You go back to looking like a man and acting like a man, and then I'll see if youre good enough to join my little group."

Somehow the Christian church has come to believe that this is the way to call people to Christ's gospel of forgiveness. They've lost sight of the fact that Jesus came to save us from ourselves. Under these circumstances would you rush to join the bandwagon?

Fortunately, II was nurtured and taught through my interaction with the people of Bill's church. They were an encouragement in developing my self confidence, and II soon knew that the time was right to be baptized and to seek church membership. II had come to realize that II was a new creation in Christ, with a completely new understanding of the place Christ had in my life.

The Sunday morning II stood in the baptismal tank in front of the whole church, II affirmed my acceptance of Christ as my personal saviour and acknowledged that He had died on the cross and rose from the dead so that II might have eternal life. To acknowledge the part the congregation played in my restoration, II recited a short rhyme:

Now Janet sat on the fence wall
and Janet had a great fall.

Then all the King's men
and all the King's women
helped put Janet together again.

Following the service a young girl and her mother approached me because the little rhyme II recited was like
another the little girl knew, and she wanted to know why
II was baptized. Now, II'm not a theological person, and
II was taken back by the sincerity of the girl's question.
How would Jesus have answered in simple language that
a child could understand? Without hesitation, the words
just seemed to fall out of my mouth. "Because Jesus did
it, and II want to be like him," II heard myself saying.
Her mother thanked me for my simple answer, and then
II watched as they walked off hand in hand, but then
the little girl stopped, turned, and gave me a big smile.
Somehow II just felt at that moment that the Holy Spirit
had planted a mustard seed in her life.

My newly acquired freedom had released me from the
prison of the closet II held in my mind. II had believed
II felt safe in there, but actually II was scared to death
of people. Now I felt free to give a person a hug, to
approach new people and ask them to join me for coffee,
for II knew how lonely it can be to walk into the midst
of people who are already friendly with one another. No
one should ever feel like a stranger in the house of the
Lord. In my past, as part of my work in corporate sales,

II was uneasy walking into 'cold' sales calls knowing that II would be confronted by people II didn't know. Now II felt that there was a magnet drawing me to those new faces. The only explanation was that the Holy Spirit was working within me to make this possible, though my old adversary, doubt, still tried to sidetrack me when II least expected.

Each spring our church sponsored a women's retreat where we could fellowship, let our hair down, converse on an emotional level, develop ourselves spiritually, and strengthen our walk with Christ. The first year that II decided to go, doubt wasn't whispering. It was yelling at me. "What on earth do you think you're doing? This is for real females. What will you ever talk about? You've never had a baby? You've never been left by a man and had to raise a family? They won't want to share a room with you." On and on my mind dwelt on these things, but II went anyway.

Unlike male retreats that are usually convened around some sports activity or and involve competitions or strategy games, this was a weekend where feelings and emotions could be shared, where support and understanding were as close as the woman next to me, where assurance and quietness were all about me. II found it to be a time of completion, where I could complete my transition into the female world by listening to the deepest emotions of the women as they opened themselves to one another and to God.

My presence gave the weekend a lighter side that year, perhaps not by design, but through the course of events. One session was about the beauty of the female body from God's perspective. We were instructed to gather in small groups of five or six and to share how our mothers had prepared us for our first menstrual period.

II had become the focus of all the groups in the room, and their beaming broad grins indicated their anticipation of how II would dig myself out of this. Then they started egging me on.

"Yes, Janet. Tell us. We're dying to know."

With mock seriousness, I admitted, "My mom was like a lot of other moms in those days. We never discussed things like that. Maybe that's why I never got mine."

We had to let the retreat leader in on the humor of the situation, because she knew nothing about my past. Being able to poke fun at myself seems to put everyone at ease when a situation comes awkward.

That weekend was a fresh start at learning the true meaning of being completely female. It's one thing to live all your life in a closet believing you are a female, but it is quite another living out of the closet and being accepted as a female. II came to realize that there are specific expectations of the female by society. The female role is simple. It is unquestionably to take care of the family and the home front. My role as a man was that of provider, and with that accomplished, II was free to pursue my interests. Now that II am a female, the shoe

222

is on the other foot. If there are dishes to do, food to prepare, children to tend, the males search out a female to take over because they say we do it better. Well fellows, practice makes perfect.

Now II have the opportunity to speak with other women on a completely different level. It is often deeply personal and implies the need of confidentiality. This is something men rarely experience, even with their closest friends. It is in these conversations that II must come to terms with that part of my past, of being thought to be male, and to comprehend the pain other women have experienced and are sharing with me because of the men in their lives. Men, let me tell you from my own first hand experience about the shear terror of being overpowered, thrown to the ground, having our clothing ripped against our flesh, and being beaten about the face and body. Why? You're not even animals. Animals are more gentle. You make us feel so dirty, a thousand showers will never remove your stench. You have stolen a part of our lives. We are not personal property. This pain so emotionally cuts and scars us that it reaches deep into our souls.

The rape, abandonment, and abuse that women have endured makes me angry with these foolish little men, but perhaps a lot of the anger can deservedly be pointed in my direction because of the insensitive and selfish attitudes that II held in my previous life with my wife, partly out of conditioned male attitudes and partly because II

223

just didn't take time to understand what my wife was trying to communicate, and now it's too late to tell her that II'm sorry.

There have been a great many books written on the differences between men and women, and undoubtedly they all have some truth, but what good are they if no one learns or tries to comprehend the other gender's role. One of the biggest differences is often the level upon which each gender communicates, feelings versus logic. The good news is that each gender can learn the language of the other by being quiet and listening. Just as when we communicate with God, sometimes we need to be quiet and listen intently to each other. In carpentry we're told to measure twice and cut once. In relationships II guess we should listen twice and speak once. II have had the opportunity to live in both genders, both in secret and openly, and hopefully from my experience there might be just one sentence, one phrase that might cause someone to say, "Now I understand."

Though my experience at the retreat had allowed me to feel fully female emotionally as well as physically, II still needed to come to terms with my feelings about intimacy and affection. This was an area of my life that had been in the deep freeze for so many years. Though II recognized it is an area in my life that needed work, II never quite got it thawed before II stuffed it back in the freezer.

The experience and thought of rejection for me was

unbearable in spite of all II had been through. As II tried to deal with this issue, II thought a female pastor could shed better light on it for me. In the process she reminded me of how to meditate and listen for the Lord to speak. II sat quietly for a period of time each day for several days expecting God to communicate in some fashion. Then one day as II sat with my eyes closed, II had a vision in my mind that appeared as clear as if II were looking out the window. Standing in front of me was a green succulent cactus about six feet tall. Around it's base was a tangle of knurled, dried up roots that twisted and intertwined around one another, so II couldn't tell where one started and one ended. As it stood silently in the blazing sun, it had the appearance of a person standing with arms reaching upward in praise.

The vision left me wondering why a person who had never seen the desert or a cactus except in a photograph would have such a vivid vision.

This sparked my curiosity to find out more about the cactus. As II read up on the cactus, II discovered that they are the storehouses of the desert. They are capable of storing up moisture from the night time dew, hence the need for massive root systems near the surface. Their stored water provides moisture for other animals. They provide protection and shade. They provide food and beauty in a barren landscape. Perhaps this is my function in life. II too like the cactus am a storehouse of God's mercies to be shared with everyone.

Now II'd like to introduce you to my friend who has stood by me through out my life. His name is Jesus. He was born of an earthly mother and a heavenly father, grew up just like you and me, as a baby, a child, a teenager and an adult. His step-dad was a carpenter and trained him to work in the family carpentry shop. That was until one day His heavenly Father called Him to begin teaching people about the love God has for all humanity, not just a select few.

For the next three years He did just that. He taught people in simple words and examples that they could understand. He underscored His authority by doing some pretty amazing things. He also condensed all the laws that people couldn't possibly keep into three simple commands: love God with every part of your being, love yourself, and love the people who come into your lives.

Of course this kind of teaching angered the existing church rulers, and for this my friend paid with his life by being nailed to a cross. Then His heavenly Father chose to reveal Himself as mightier than death, so after three days He raised His Son from the grave and offered every person, with no ifs ands or buts, who believe in Jesus and are willing to let Him direct their lives, the free gift of knowing that when they die they will live forever with God.

Today my friend lives in heaven with His Father. What do you say? Are you ready to receive His love and His freedom from oppression, to accept His free gift.

He's standing there beside you right now. The choice is yours. Just tell him you accept His love. It's that simple. God is the master of simplicity.

16
A Little Child Shall Lead Them

II believe the most appropriate way to end this story is through the wisdom of a child, my grandson, who wrote his own account about my life from his point of view. Only through the simplicity and honesty of a child can the real meaning be grasped from all that II have tried to explain in a much more complicated way. Perhaps the generations to follow will be able to eliminate the discrimination and ridicule that occurs because people have a different lifestyle or have warts on their noses.

Change is a part of life.
In nature, the seasons change.

Animals change too.
Puppies grow into dogs.
But they're still animals.

People change in a lot of ways.
They might change their hair,
their jobs, their friends,

their hobbies.
They might learn new things
or become handicapped.
People change all the time.

My poppy changed a lot in some ways.
In other ways he stayed the same.
But he's still a person.
And he's still a part of our family.

These are the ways poppy changed:
he wears different clothes,
he lives in a different place,
he had an operation.

These are the ways he stayed the same:
he still loves me,
he still loves his family,
he is still a good artist and a good carpenter.

One thing that hasn't changed
is my feeling for poppy.

I still love him.